Logical Lyrics

From Philosophy to Poetics

Texts in Computing
Volume 1
Programming Languages and Operational Semantics
Maribel Fernandez

Volume 2
An Introduction to Lambda Calculi for Computer Scientists
Chris Hankin

Volume 3
Introduction to Logic
Rob Nederpelt and Fairouz Kamareddine

Volume 4
The Haskell Road to Logic, Maths and Programming
Kees Doets and Jan van Eijck

Volume 6
Bridges from Classical to Nonmonotonic Logic
David Makinson

Texts in Algorithmics
Volume 1
Handbook of String Matching Algorithms
Thierry Lecroq and Christian Charras, eds

Volume 2
String Algorithmics
Costas Iliopoulos and Thierry Lecroq, eds

Volume 3
Algorithms & Computational Methods for Biochemical and Evolutionary Networks
Katia Guimaraes and Marie-France Sagot, eds

Laws and Models in Science
Donald Gillies, ed

Feisty Fragments for Philosophy
Vincent Hendricks

The Honorary Survivor
Ben Lappin

Logical Lyrics

From Philosophy to Poetics

Vincent F. Hendricks

ISBN 1-904-987-04-4
King's College Publications
Scientific Director: Dov Gabbay
Managing Director: Jane Spurr
Department of Computer Science
Strand, London WC2R 2LS, UK
kcp@dcs.kcl.ac.uk
www.dcs.kcl.ac.uk/kcl-publications/

Cover design by Richard Fraser, www.avalonarts.co.uk
Interior illustrations by Vincent F. Hendricks
Printed by Lightning Source, Milton Keynes, UK

To my brother

Angelo M. Irizarry

Contents

Preface

Logic is the study of valid inferences and arguments. It has been around ever since man could reason. Academically it is commonly viewed as an appendix to philosophy, or situated in a grey-zone between philosophy and mathematics which are generally conceived as highly theoretical and abstract disciplines. Logic also rears its head in more practical areas ranging from computer science via psychology, linguistics and rhetorics, to economics and politics. In natural science, social science and the humanities logic is around.

Every day logic surrounds us. Used and abused at cocktail parties and dinner functions, in friendly conversations and verbal feuds, in thinking and reflecting, logic is a tool of mind. It is the language of thought. Logic is part of the human condition, and concerns us all even if it is not always used by man. Considered familiar and natural when understood as synonymous with 'common-sense', 'sure', 'of course', and 'that's obvious', logic is at the same time considered alien – perhaps even boring and dry – when used in science. Logic then transforms into strange symbols, complicated formulae, Greek letters, technical illustrations, algebras and numbers, propositions, lemmata and theorems ... things out of a math-book rather than your thoughts.

Logic doesn't care about labels like alien. It is about the structure of language rather than its content, and the ways we reason rather than what we reason about. Snap reasoning, witty questions, and fast responses are admirable qualities to have, but they do not necessarily have anything to do with logic. Elaborations, extensive arguments and tedious proofs are needed because our ways of thinking can get so complicated at times that we can't be snappy, witty or speedy without the symbols. And while bringing rigor and system to our reasoning, many of the symbols, formulae and letters are visually fascinating constructions and aesthetically pleasing.

Aristotle once said that contradicting yourself you are nothing but a plant, and catching others in a contradiction we will be the first to point out the inconsistency. Complicated formal proofs can be fascinating and exciting, if for no other reason because they convey something about how far we can *validly* get with our minds. Validity in reasoning is not only an admirable quality, it is one of the defining features of reason. Enjoy the book.

Logical Lyrics: From Philosophy to Poetics is an independent follow-up to *Feisty Fragments: For Philosophy* which is a collection of critical citations, funny aphorisms, and inquisitive quotations about philosophy and philosophers from all sorts of people. *Logical Lyrics* is a collection of citations, aphorisms and quotations dedicated to logic rather than philosophy.

Many of the quotes in *Logical Lyrics* have been suggested by working logicians reflecting on their own subject matter. This book may be seen as a critical, funny and inquisitive field report written by the practitioners of logic. They come from all over the world; they quote other logicians as well as playwrights and poets, rock-stars and pop-bands. From the premisses to the conclusion, *Logical Lyrics: From Philosophy to Poetics* simply proves the relevance of logic to our existence.

$\exists$

I would like to acknowledge colleagues, associates and friends who have suggested citations and quotes included in *Logical Lyrics*. In particular I would like to extend my gratitude to members of ΦLOG – The Network for Philosophical Logic and Its Applications and ΦNEWS – The Newsletter for Philosophical Logic and Its Applications who have kindly contributed their favorite quotes on logic, logicians and logical matters. All contributors are listed in a separate section below.

I would like to thank Johan van Benthem, Brian F. Chellas, Solomon Feferman, Jaakko Hintikka, David Makinson, John Sowa and John Symons for their encouragement and support. Pelle Guldborg Hansen kindly assisted me in tracking down copyright holders and helped me with the permissions logistics.

I am indebted to all the publishers, literary agents and executors, copyright holders, permissions- and rights-executives for allowing me to quote material used in *Logical Lyrics*. A separate detailed Acknowledgements section is provided at the end of the book.

I would like to thank my proof-reader Henriette Holm and my New York City-mom Mimi Vang Olsen. My gratitude finally goes out to King's College Publications, in particular Scientific Director Prof. Dov M. Gabbay, Managing Director Jane Spurr, and Editorial Assistant Anna Maros.

—Vincent F. Hendricks
January 2005
New York City

Disclaimer

Material for *Logical Lyrics: From Philosophy to Poetics* has – besides from kind direct contributions from ΦLOG-members and ΦNEWS-subscribers – been taken from all over; books, articles, TV- and radio-shows, the internet etc. Texts have sometimes been corrupt and references have been missing but all possible attempts have been made to reconstruct and track down as much and as many as possible and seek permission to quote. Where references are missing, the quotes may be considered attributed. Full apologies are granted for any errors and omissions. There are instances where it has been impossible to trace the copyright holders. If notified of any error or omission it will be rectified at the earliest opportunity.

The copyright holders who have explicitly requested a particular credit line immediately after the quoted material have been honored, but otherwise credits are to be found in the Bibliography and Acknowledgements sections. All the quotations suggested by ΦLOG-members and ΦNEWS-subscribers are followed by a credit line to the suggestor.

—Vincent F. Hendricks
January 2005
New York City

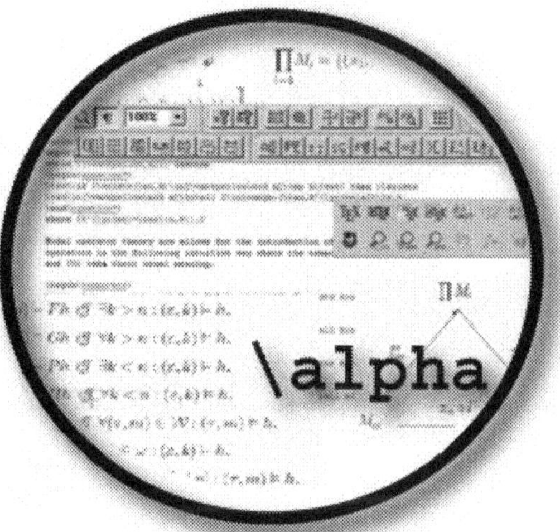

Joseph Addison

⊢ 1672—1719 *English essayist, poet and statesman*

If we may believe our logicians, man is distinguished from all other creatures by the faculty of laughter. —[1]

Nothing that isn't a real crime makes a man appear so contemptible and little in the eyes of the world as inconsistency. —[1]

Suggested by David Makinson

Alan Ross Anderson

⊢ 1925—1973 *American logician and philosopher*

All logic manuscripts contain infinitely many errors. Proof: For every error you find there is another one.

Suggested by Joao Marcos

Alan Ross Anderson & Nuel D. Belnap, Jr.

⊢ *American logicians and philosophers*

... we should be delighted if someone were to read this book just for the jokes ... —[2]: xxiii

Suggested by Stig Alstrup Rasmussen

Marian Anderson

⊢ 1897—1993 *American contralto and opera singer*

Fear is a disease that eats away at logic and makes man inhuman. —[3]

Oswald de Andreade

⊢ 1890—1954 *Brazilian poet, playwright, novelist and social agitator*

But we never admitted the birth of logic among us. —[4]

Suggested by Joao Marcos

† Anonymous

A minister was talking to a group of young children. 'Who can tell me what we must do before we can expect forgiveness of sin?' There was a moment's pause, then Tommy made a logical contribution: 'Well, sir, first we have got to sin.'

Through logic and inference we can prove anything. Therefore, logic and inference, in contrast to ordinary daily living experience, are secondary instruments of knowledge. Probably tertiary.

Zen: the sound of the ax chopping. Chopping logic.

There is science, logic, reason; there is thought verified by experience. And then there is California.

Logic is a systematic method of coming to the wrong conclusion with confidence.

When intuition and logic agree, you are always right.

Logic turns pessimistic the idiot.

Only one thing is certain—that is, nothing is certain. If this statement is true, it is also false.

A trial is still an ordeal by battle. For the broad-sword there is the weight of evidence; for the battle-ax the force of logic; for the sharp spear, the blazing gleam of truth; for the rapier, the quick and flashing knife of wit. (attributed Lloyd Paul Stryker)

We live in a Newtonian world of Einsteinian physics ruled by Frankenstein logic. (attributed David Russell)

Drama is imagination limited by logic. Mathematics is logic limited by imagination. (attributed Nathan Campbell)

In elementary school, in case of fire you have to line up quietly in a single file line from smallest to tallest. What is the logic? Do tall people burn slower? (attributed Warren Hutcherson)

Life would have no consequence,
If all I saw made perfect sense.
Life would not be magical,
If all I saw was logical.
So I question all I see,
To try and solve the mystery.
I've been living under delusion,
Led astray by my confusion.

The decision doesn't have to be logical, it was unanimous.

The fact that logic cannot satisfy us awakens an almost insatiable hunger for the irrational. (attributed A.N. Wilson)

Man always has two reasons for the things he does; the logical one and the real one.

An economist, a logician, and a mathematician are riding in a train. Just after they have crossed the border into Scotland, they see through the window a brown cow standing parallel to the train.
The economist says, 'Look, cows in Scotland are brown.'
The logician says, 'No, there are cows in Scotland of which at least one is brown.'
The mathematician says, 'No, there is at least one cow in Scotland, of which one side appears to be brown.'

The primary purpose of the DATA statement is to give names to constants; instead of referring to pi as 3.141592653589793 at every appearance, the variable PI can be given that value with a DATA statement and used instead of the longer form of the constant. This also simplifies modifying the program, should the value of pi change. [Fortran manual for Xerox computers]

If you go in for argument, take care of your temper. Your logic, if you have any, will take care of itself. (attributed Joseph Farrell)

In Woolstonecraft's page, BRIDGET
BEARWELL was skilld
And her fancy with novel inventions was
filld
But Bridget improvd on Miss Wool-
stonecrafts plan,
And projected some small revolution in
man.
Tis plain, she exclaimd, that the
sexes should share,
In each others employments, amusements and care.
I'm taught in man's duties and honors
to join,
And, therefore, let man be partaker of mine:
Since to share with my husband in logic
Im fit
In classical lore, mathematics, and wit;
In return, he shall yield the pot, kettle,
and ladle,
And unite in the charge of the kitchen
and cradle. —[5]

Eggheads unite! You got nothing to lose but your yolks! (attributed Adlai Stevenson)

Major paradoxes provide food for logical thought for decades and sometimes centuries. (attributed Nicholas Bourbaki)

St. Thomas Aquinas

⊢ 1225—1274 *Italian philosopher*

Logic is the science and art which directs the act of the reason, by which a man in the exercise of his reason is enabled to proceed without error, confusion, or unnecessary difficulty. —[6]: lect. i, I, 138

Louis Aragon

⊢ 1897—1982 *French poet, novelist and essayist*

I demand that my books be judged with utmost severity, by knowledgeable people who know the rules of grammar and of logic, and who will seek beneath the footsteps of my commas the lice of my thought in the head of my style. —[7]

Aristotle

⊢ 384—322 BC *Greek philosopher*

This, then, is the most certain of all principles, since it answers to the definition given above. For it is impossible for any one to believe the same thing to be and not to be, as some think

Heraclitus says. For what a man says, he does not necessarily believe; and if it is impossible that contrary attributes should belong at the same time to the same subject (the usual qualifications must be presupposed in this premiss too), and if an opinion which contradicts another is contrary to it, obviously it is impossible for the same man at the same time to believe the same thing to be and not to be; for if a man were mistaken on this point he would have contrary opinions at the same time. It is for this reason that all who are carrying out a demonstration reduce it to this as an ultimate belief; for this is naturally the starting-point even for all the other axioms. —[8]

Probable impossibilities are to be preferred to improbable possibilities. —[9]: 24, 1460a

Suggested by David Makinson

Roger Ascham

⊢ 1515—1568 *English humanist and scholar*

Mark all mathematical heads which be wholly and only bent on these sciences, how solitary they be themselves, how unfit to live with others, how unapt to serve the world. —[10]

Isaac Asimov

⊢ 1920—1992 *American science-fiction writer*

Those people who think they know everything are a great annoyance to those of us who do.

The young specialist in English Lit, ... lectured me severely on the fact that in every century people have thought they understood the Universe at last, and in every century they were proved to be wrong. It follows that the one thing we can say about our modern 'knowledge' is that it is wrong. —[11]

... My answer to him was, '... when people thought the Earth was flat, they were wrong. When people thought the Earth was spherical they were wrong. But if you think that thinking the Earth is spherical is just as wrong as thinking the Earth is flat, then your view is wronger than both of them put together.' —[11]: 226

Justin Brooks Atkinson

⊢ 1894—1984 *American drama critic and journalist*

The humorous man recognizes that absolute purity, absolute justice, absolute logic and perfection are beyond human achievement and that men have been able to live happily for thousands of years in a state of genial frailty. —[12]

Charles Babbage

⊢ 1792—1891 *English 'father of computing'*

Errors using inadequate data are much less than those using no data at all.

Francis Bacon

⊢ 1561—1626 *English lawyer, statesman and philosopher*

If a man will begin with certainties, he shall end in doubts; but if he will be content to begin with doubts, he shall end in certainties. —[13]: v. 8

Suggested by David Makinson

Honoré de Balzac

⊢ 1799—1850 *French journalist and writer*

This coffee plunges into the stomach ... the mind is aroused, and ideas pour forth like the battalions of the Grand Army on the field of battle ... Memories charge at full gallop ... the light of comparisons deploys itself magnificently; the artillery of logic hurry in with their train of ammunition; flashes of wit pop up like sharp-shooters.

Dave Barry

⊢ *American humor columnist*

The world is full of strange phenomena that cannot be explained by the laws of logic or science. Dennis Rodman is only one example. —[15]

Jon Barwise

⊢ 1942—2000 *American logician*

As logicians, we do our subject a disservice by convincing others that logic is first-order, and then convincing them that almost none of the concepts of modern mathematics can really be captured in first-order logic. —[16]

Suggested by Joao Marcos

Isaac Bashevis

⊢ 1904—1991 *Polish-born, American journalist and novelist*

They still believe in God, the family, angels, witches, goblins, logic, clarity, punctuation, and other obsolete stuff. —[17]

Simone de Beauvoir

⊢ 1908—1986 *French existentialist and writer*

In masculine hands logic is often a form of violence, a sly kind of tyranny. —[18]

Lyman Beecher

⊢ 1775—1863 *American minister*

Eloquence is logic on fire. —[19]

Johan van Benthem

⊢ 1949— *Dutch logician and philosopher*

Logic may not really be empirical cognitive science of reasoning and interaction (facts are strong medicine ...): but its inspiration for new theory building certainly derives from observations about natural logic and actual human behavior. —[20]: 52

Yogi Berra

⊢ 1925— *American baseball player*

In theory there is no difference between theory and practice. In practice there is.

Suggested by Achille Varzi

Bernard Berenson

⊢ 1865—1959 *American art critic and writer*

Consistency requires you to be as ignorant today as you were a year ago. —[21]

Ambrose Bierce

⊢ 1842—1914 *American journalist*

LOGIC, n. The art of thinking and reasoning in strict accordance with the limitations and incapacities of the human misunderstanding. —[22]

Suggested by George Englebretsen

The basic of logic is the syllogism, consisting of a major and a minor premise and a conclusion – thus:

Major Premise: Sixty men can do a piece of work sixty times as quickly as one man.

Minor Premise: One man can dig a posthole in sixty seconds; therefore –

Conclusion: Sixty men can dig a posthole in one second.

This may be called the syllogism arithmetical, in which, by combining logic and mathematics, we obtain a double certainty and are twice blessed. —[22]

SYLLOGISM, n. A logical formula consisting of a major and a minor assumption and an inconsequent. (See LOGIC) —[22]

Matt Biershbach

⊢ *American computer scientist*

People that think logically are a nice contrast to the real world.

Niels Bohr

⊢ 1885—1965 *Danish physicist*

No, no, you're not thinking; you're just being logical. —[23]

How wonderful that we have met with a paradox. Now we have some hope of making progress. —[23]

Ludwig Boltzmann

⊢ 1844—1906 *German physicist*

The most ordinary things are to philosophy a source of insoluble puzzles. With infinite ingenuity it constructs a concept of space or time and then finds it absolutely impossible that there be objects in this space or that processes occur during this time ... the source of this kind of logic lies in excessive confidence in the so-called laws of thought. —[24]: 7

Napoleon Bonaparte

⊢ 1769—1821 *French emperor*

A mathematician of the first rank, Laplace quickly revealed himself as only a mediocre administrator; from his first work we saw that we had been deceived. Laplace saw no question from its true point of view; he sought subtleties everywhere; had only doubtful ideas, and finally carried the spirit of the infinitely small into administration.

Edward de Bono

⊢ 1933— *Maltese educator*

Most of the mistakes in thinking are inadequacies of perception rather than mistakes of logic. —[25]

Victor Borge

⊢ 1909—2000 *Danish comedian*

Humor [is] something that thrives between man's aspirations and his limitations. There is more logic in humor than in anything else. Because, you see, humor is truth. —[26]

Pierre Bourdieu

⊢ 1930—2002 *French philosopher*

Practice has a logic which is not that of the logician. —[27]: 86

Reprinted by the kind permission of Les Editions de Minuit

Rita Mae Brown

⊢ 1944— *American author and social activist*

Intuition is a suspension of logic due to impatience. —[28]

If the world were a logical place, men would ride side-saddle. —[28]

Charlotte Brönte

⊢ 1816—1855 *English writer*

Better to be without logic than without feeling. —[29]

Jean de la Bruyére

⊢ 1645—1696 *French writer*

Logic is the technique by which we add conviction to truth. —[30]

Edmund Burke

⊢ 1729—1797 *English statesman, parliamentary orator and political thinker*

Example is the school of mankind, and they will learn at no other. —[31]: Letters on a Regicide Peace (1795–7)

Suggested by John Sowa

Daniel H. Burnham

⊢ 1846—1912 *American architect and city planner*

Make no little plans. They have no magic to stir men's blood and probably themselves will not be realized. Make big plans. Aim high in hope and work. Remembering that a noble, logical diagram once recorded will not die.

George W. Bush, Jr.

⊢ 1946— *43rd American president*

I know what I believe. I will continue to articulate what I believe and what I believe. I believe what I believe is right. —[32]

Suggested by John Sowa

Vannevar Bush

⊢ 1890—1974 *American engineer*

If scientific reasoning were limited to the logical processes of arithmetic, we should not get very far in our understanding of the physical world. One might as well attempt to grasp the game of poker entirely by the use of the mathematics of probability. —[33]

Samuel Butler

⊢ 1612—1680 *English writer*

Logic is like the sword—those who appeal to it shall perish by it. —[34]

No mistake is more common and more fatuous than appealing to logic in cases which are beyond her jurisdiction. —[34]

He was in Logic a great critic,
Profoundly skill'd in Analytic;
He could distinguish, and divide
A hair 'twixt south and south-west side.
—[35]: pt. I, canto I, l. 65

Life is the art of drawing sufficient conclusions from insufficient premises. —[34]

Suggested by David Makinson

Thomas Carlyle

⊢ 1795—1881 *Scottish historian and sociological writer*

High Air-castles are cunningly built of Words, the Words well bedded also in good Logic-mortar; wherein, however, no Knowledge will come to lodge. —[37]: bk. I, ch. VIII

The meaning of song goes deep. Who in logical words can explain the effect music has on us? A kind of inarticulate, unfathomable speech, which leads us to the edge of the infinite, and lets us for a moment gaze into that!

Rudolf Carnap

⊢ 1891—1970 *German-born, American philosopher*

Logic is not concerned with human behavior in the same sense that physiology, psychology, and social sciences are concerned with it. These sciences formulate laws or universal statements which have as their subject matter human activities as processes in time. Logic, on the contrary, is concerned with relations between factual sentences (or thoughts). If logic ever discusses the truth of factual sentences it does so only conditionally, somewhat as follows: If such-and-such a sentence is true, then such-and-such another sentence is true. Logic itself does not decide whether the first sentence is true, but surrenders that question to one or the other of the empirical sciences. —[38]

Dale Carnegie

⊢ 1888—1955 *American writer and educator*

When dealing with people, let us remember we are not dealing with creatures of logic. We are dealing with creatures of emotion, creatures bustling with prejudices and motivated by pride and vanity. —[39]

Lewis Carroll

⊢ 1832—1898 *English writer and mathematician*

'Contrariwise,' continued Tweedledee, 'if it was so, it might be; and if it were so, it would be; but as it isn't, it ain't. That's logic.' —[41]: 165

Suggested by Aaron Hunter and Joao Marcos

Once master the machinery of Symbolic Logic, and you have a mental occupation always at hand, of absorbing interest, and one that will be of real use to you in any subject you may take up. It will give you clearness of thought – the ability to see your way through a puzzle – the habit of arranging your ideas in an orderly and get-at-able form – and, more valuable than all, the power to detect fallacies, and to tear to pieces the flimsy arguments, which you will so continually encounter in books, in newspapers, in speeches, and even in sermons, and which so easily delue those who have never taken the trouble to amster this fascinating Art. —[41]: 1119 (originally in *Symbolic Logic*)

Suggested by Aaron Hunter

'For a complete logical argument,' Arthur began with admirable solemnity, 'we need two prim Misses—'

'Of course!' she interrupted. 'I remember that word now. And they produce — ?'

'A Delusion,' said Arthur.

'Ye–es?' she said dubiously. 'I don't seem to remember that so well.

But what is the whole argument called?'

'A Sillygism?'

'Ah, yes! I remember now. But I don't need a Sillygism, you know, to prove that mathematical axiom you mentioned.'

'Nor to prove that 'all angles are equal', I suppose?'

'Why, of course not! One takes such a simple truth as that for granted!' —[41]: 388 (originally in *Sylvie and Bruno*)

Suggested by Aaron Hunter

Logic will take you by the throat and force you to agree! —[40]

Suggested by George Englebretsen

Whatever Logic is good enough to tell me is worth writing down.—[40]

Suggested by George Englebretsen

Campos de Carvalho

⊢ 1928— *Brazilian economist*

I killed my logic teacher when I was 16. Allegedly self-defense – and what defense would be more legitimate? – I managed to be absolved by five votes against two, and I went to live under a bridge of the Seine, though I have never been in Paris. —[42]

Suggested by Joao Marcos

C.C. Chang & H. Jerome Keisler

⊢ *American logicians*

For the amusement of all those who gave us help, we dedicate our book to all model theorists who have never dedicated a book to themselves. —[43]: vi

Suggested by Stig Alstrup Rasmussen

G.K. Chesterton

⊢ 1874—1936 *English writer*

Poets do not go mad; but chess-players do. Mathematicians go mad, and cashiers; but creative artists very seldom. I am not, as will be seen, in any sense attacking logic: I only say that this danger does lie in logic, not in imagination. —[46]: ch. 2

The poet only asks to get his head into the heavens. It is the logician who seeks to get the heavens into his head. And it is his head that splits. —[46]: ch. 2

Truths turn into dogmas the moment they are disputed. —[44]

Suggested by Joao Marcos

You can only find truth with logic if you have already found truth without it. —[45]

Suggested by Joao Marcos and John Symons

The Renaissance was, as much as anything, a revolt from the logic of the Middle Ages. We speak of the Renaissance as the birth of rationalism; it was in many ways the birth of irrationalism. It is true that the medieval Schoolmen, who had produced the finest logic that the world has ever seen, had in later years produced more logic than the world can ever be expected to stand. They had loaded and lumbered up the world with libraries of mere logic; and some effort was bound to be made to free it from such endless chains of deduction. Therefore, there was in the Renaissance a wild touch of revolt, not against religion but against reason ... When all is said, there is something a little sinister in the number of mad people in Shakespeare. We say that he uses his fools to brighten the dark background of tragedy; I think he sometimes uses them to darken it. —[47]

Helena Christensen

⊢ 1968— *Danish super-model*

In modelling, there is no point in trying to prove you have a brain, so why even bother? I'd sooner save the energy for something more meaningful.

Agatha Christie

⊢ 1890—1976 *English detective story writer*

How much do we know at any time?
Much more, or so I believe, than we know we know! —[48]

Suggested by John Sowa

Winston Churchill

⊢ 1874—1965 *English prime minister*

Logic is a poor guide compared with custom.

We must beware of needless innovations, especially when guided by logic. —[49]

... man will occasionally stumble over the truth, but usually manages to pick himself up, walk over or around it, and carry on. —[50]

Auguste Comte

⊢ 1798—1857 *French philosopher*

As far as deduction prevails over induction, the spirit will remain inclined toward metaphysical speculations. —[53]: I, 177

Suggested by John Sowa

Samuel Taylor Coleridge

⊢ 1772—1834 *English poet*

Poetry, even that of the loftiest, and seemingly, that of the wildest odes, [has] a logic of its own as severe as that of science; and more difficult, because more subtle, more complex, and dependent on more and more fugitive causes. In the truly great poets ... there is a reason assignable, not only for every word, but for the position of every word.

Charles Caleb Colton

⊢ 1780—1832 *English sportsman and writer*

Man is an embodied paradox, a bundle of contradictions. —[52]

Suggested by David Makinson

Logic is a large drawer, containing some useful instruments, and many more that are superfluous. A wise man will look into it for two purposes, to avail himself of those instruments that are really useful, and to admire the ingenuity with which those that are not so, are assorted and arranged. —[52]

Joseph Conrad

⊢ 1780—1832 *English novelist*

A droll thing life is—that mysterious arrangement of merciless logic for a futile purpose. The most you can hope from it is some knowledge of yourself and that comes too late.

Mason Cooley

⊢ 1927— *American aphorist*

Logic teaches rules for presentation, not thinking.
—[54]: Seventh Selection

Our punning minds rejoin what logic has separated.
—[54]: Fifth Selection

Logic and fact keep interfering with the easy flow of conversation. —[54]

Jacques Cousteau

⊢ 1910—1997 *French documentary filmmaker, ocean explorer and oceanographer*

If we were logical, the future would be bleak indeed. But we are more than logical. We are human beings, and we have faith, and we have hope and we can work.

Mandell Creighton

⊢ 1843—1901 *English bishop*

All true knowledge contradicts commonsense.

4 D

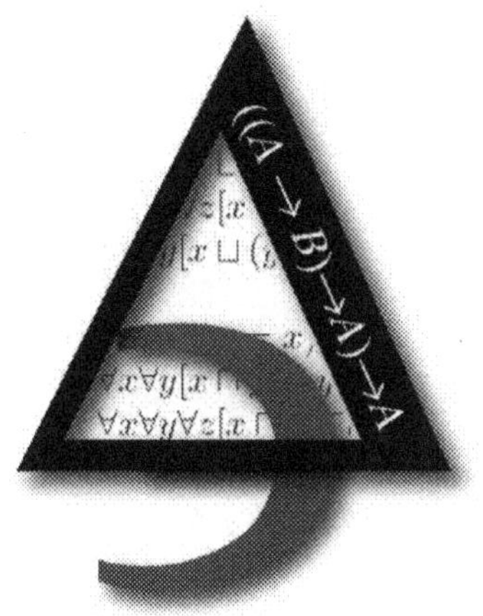

Pierre Dac

⊢ 1893—1975 *French humorist*

A false error is not necessarily a genuine truth. —[55]

Suggested by Joao Marcos

If in pure reality it is always right not to be wrong, in altered reality it is often wrong to be right. —[55]

Suggested by Joao Marcos

Max Wilhelm Dehn

⊢ 1878—1952 *German-American mathematician*

Pure mathematics is, in its way, the poetry of logical ideas. —[56]: vol. 5, no. 2

Democritus

⊢ ca 420 BC *Greek philosopher*

We know nothing in reality; for truth lies in an abyss.

Daniel C. Dennett

⊢ 1942— *American philosopher*

There's nothing I like less than bad arguments for a view that I hold dear.

Depeche Mode

⊢ *English pop-band*

Now you're standing there tongue tied
You'd better learn your lesson well
Hide what you have to hide
And tell what you have to tell
You'll see your problems multiplied
If you continually decide
To faithfully pursue
The policy of truth. —[57]: Policy of Truth

Lyrics by Martin Gore

Robert Devereux

⊢ 1566—1601 *Earl of Essex*

Reasons are not like garments, the worse for wearing.

Suggested by David Makinson

John Dewey

⊢ 1859—1952 *American philosopher*

Man is not logical and his intellectual history is a record of mental reserves and compromises. He hangs on to what he can in his old beliefs even when he is compelled to surrender their logical basis. —[58]

Edsger W. Dijkstra

⊢ 1930—2002 *American computer scientist*

Formulae have always frightened me. They frightened me, I remember, when I was sixteen and had bought my books for the next year. I was particularly alarmed by my new book on trigonometry, full of sines, cosines, and Greek letters, and asked my mother a gifted mathematician whether trigonometry was difficult. I gratefully acknowledge her wise answer:

> 'Oh, no. Know your formulae, and always remember that you are on the wrong track when you need more than five lines.'

In retrospect, I think that no other advice has had such a profound influence on my way of working.

And even now, my first reaction to formulae, written by someone else, is one of repulsion – in particular when an unfamiliar notational convention is used – and when reading an article, my natural reaction is to skip the formulae. —[59]

Suggested by John Sowa

At the same time, I have a warm appreciation for well-designed formalisms that enable me to do things that I couldn't possibly do without them. —[59]

Suggested by John Sowa

Benjamin Disraeli

⊢ 1804—1881 *English prime minister*

A consistent man believes in destiny, a capricious man in chance.

Fyodor Dostoevsky

⊢ 1821—1881 *Russian writer*

Man has such a predilection for systems and abstract deductions that he is ready to distort the truth intentionally, he is ready to deny the evidence of his senses only to justify his logic. —[60]

Theodore M. Drange

⊢ 1934— *American philosopher*

Some methodological atheists formulate the principle by saying that the burden of proof is always on any person making an existence claim, since, from a logical point of view, existence claims are only capable of proof, not disproof. No one has ever proven the nonexistence of Santa Claus, or elves, or unicorns, or anything else, simply because the very logic of an unrestricted existential proposition prohibits its disproof. It is impossible to go all over the universe and show that, for example, there are no elves anywhere. For this reason, rational methodology calls for us to deny the existence of all those things which have never been shown to exist. That is why we all regard it rational to deny the existence of Santa Claus, elves, unicorns, etc. And since God is in that same category, having never been shown to exist, it follows that rational methodology calls for us to deny the existence of God. —[64]

Nonbelief & Evil: Two Arguments for the Nonexistence of God, by Theodore M. Drange (Amherst, NY: Prometheus Books). Published in 1998

Roger Ebert

⊢ 1942— *American writer and journalist*

What makes us men is that we can think logically. What makes us human is that we sometimes choose not to.
—[65]: August 11, 1993

Tryon Edwards

⊢ 1809—1894 *American author*

Prejudices are rarely overcome by argument; not being founded in reason they cannot be destroyed by logic.

Albert Einstein

⊢ 1879—1955 *German-Swiss-American physicist*

Logic will get you from A to B. Imagination will take you everywhere. —[66]

The grand aim of all science is to cover the greatest number of empirical facts by logical deduction from the smallest number of hypotheses or axioms. —[67]

The intuitive mind is a sacred gift, the rational mind is a faithful servant. We have created a society that honors the servant and has forgotten the gift. —[66]

I think and think for months and years. Ninety-nine times, the conclusion is false. The hundreth time I am right.

Ralph Waldo Emerson

⊢ 1803—1882 *American essayist and poet*

We want in every man a long logic; we cannot pardon the absence of it, but it must not be spoken. Logic is the procession or proportionate unfolding of the intuition; but its virtue is as silent method; the moment it would appear as propositions and have a separate value, it is worthless. —[68]: Intellect

I hate quotations. —[68]: Journals, May 1849

Suggested by David Makinson

Paul Erdös

⊢ 1913—1996 *Hungarian mathematician*

A mathematician is a machine for turning coffee into theorems.

Euripides

⊢ 485—406 BC *Greek tragic poet and dramatist*

Money is far more persuasive than logical arguments.

Edward Everett

⊢ 1794—1865 *American politician and scholar*

In the pure mathematics we contemplate absolute truths which existed in the divine mind before the morning stars sang together, and which will continue to exist there when the last of their radiant host shall have fallen from heaven.

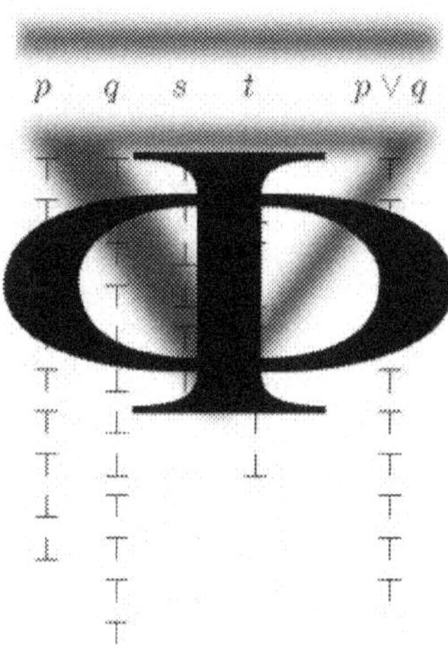

Eva Figes

⊢ 1932— *English author*

The much vaunted male logic isn't logical, because they display prejudices – against half the human race – that are considered prejudices according to any dictionary definition. —[69]

Oscar W. Firkins

⊢ 1864—1932 *American poet*

The strictly logical mind is usually if not always at fault in its valuations of that defiantly illogical thing known as human nature. —[70]

Antony Flew

⊢ 1923— *English philosopher*

In the ordinary, everyday understandings of the words involved, to say that someone survived death is to contradict yourself; while to assert that all of us live forever is to assert a manifest falsehood, the flat contrary of a universally known truth: namely, the truth that all human beings are mortal. For when, after some disaster, the 'dead' and the 'survivors' have both been listed, what logical space remains for a third category? —[71]

Bernard Le Bovier Fontenelle

⊢ 1657—1757 *French scientist and writer*

Leibniz never married; he had considered it at the age of fifty; but the person he had in mind asked for time to reflect. This gave Leibniz time to reflect, too, and so he never married.

E.M. Forster

⊢ 1879—1970 *English author and critic*

Another distinguished critic has agreed with Gide—that old lady in the anecdote who was accused by her niece of being illogical. For some time she could not be brought to understand what logic was, and when she grasped its true nature she was not so much angry as contemptuous. 'Logic! Good gracious! What rubbish!' she exclaimed. 'How can I tell what I think till I see what I say?' Her nieces, educated young women, thought that she was passée; she was really more up-to-date than they were. —[72]: 101

Suggested by John Symons

Bas van Fraassen

⊢ 1941— *French-born, American philosopher*

Certain issues in philosophy of science (having to do with observation and the definition of a theory's empirical import) had been misconstrued as issues in philosophy of logic and of language. With respect to modality, I hold the exact opposite: important philosophical problems concerning language have been misconstrued as relating to the content of science and the nature of the world. —[73]: 196

Gottlob Frege

⊢ 1848—1925 *German logician*

Your discovery of the contradiction caused me the greatest surprise and, I would almost say, consternation, since it has shaken the basis on which I intended to build my arithmetic. [...] It is all the more serious since, with the loss of my rule *V*, not only the foundations of my arithmetic, but also the sole possible foundations of arithmetic seem to vanish. — [74]: 127

Suggested by Joao Marcos

I hope I may claim in the present work to have made it probable that the laws of arithmetic are analytic judgements and consequently a priori. Arithmetic thus becomes simply a development of logic, and every proposition of arithmetic a law of logic, albeit a derivative one. To apply arithmetic in the physical sciences is to bring logic to bear on observed facts; calculation becomes deduction. —[75]: 99

If someone wants to say the same today as he expressed yesterday using the word 'today', he must replace this word with 'yesterday'. —[76]: 522

Suggested by Paul Dekker

To a mind concerned with what is beautiful in language what is indifferent to the logician can appear as just what is important. —[76]: 518

Neither logic nor mathematics has the task of investigating minds and the contents of conciousness whose bearer is a single person. Perhaps their task could be represented rather as the investigation of the mind, of the mind not of minds. —[76]: 530

Harvey Friedman

⊢ *American logician and philosopher*

To avoid confusion, I draw a distinction between foundations of mathematics and mathematical logic. The latter consists of various mathematical spin-offs from foundations of mathematics, where one deemphasizes foundational thinking, and emphasizes mathematical adventures, including connections with various branches of mathematics. —[77]: January 20, 2004

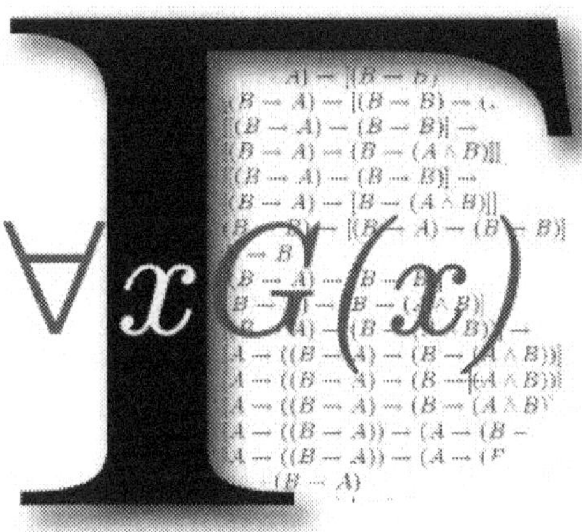

Dov M. Gabbay

⊢ 1945— *English logician and logic entrepreneur*

I am a logic. —[78]: Introduction

Karl Friedrich Gauss

⊢ 1777—1855 *German mathematician*

I have had my results for a long time, but I do not yet know how to arrive at them.

I mean the word proof not in the sense of the lawyers, who set two half proofs equal to a whole one, but in the sense of a mathematician, where half proof = 0, and it is demanded for proof that every doubt becomes impossible.

Peter Geach

⊢ *English philosopher*

Logic is unproductive like book-keeping, but without sound accountancy a productive business may smash. —[79]: 100

Suggested by George Englebretsen

Josiah Willard Gibbs

⊢ 1839—1903 *American theoretical physicist*

Mathematics is a language.

One of the principal objects of theoretical research in my department of knowledge is to find the point of view from which the subject appears in its greatest simplicity.

William Ewart Gladstone

⊢ 1809—1898 *English statesman*

Men are apt to mistake the strength of their feeling for the strength of their argument. The heated mind resents the chill touch and relentless scrutiny of logic.

Johan Wolfgang Goethe

⊢ 1749—1832 *German writer and dramatist*

All consistency leads to the Devil.

Suggested by Johan van Benthem

Collegium Logicum.

Suggested by Johan van Benthem

It is always better to say right out what you think without trying to prove anything much: For all our proofs are only variations of our opinions, and the contrary-minded listen neither to one nor the other.

Sameness leaves us in peace but it is contradiction that makes us productive. —[80]: March 28, 1827

Suggested by Joao Marcos

You accuse a woman of wavering affections, but don't blame her; she is just looking for a consistent man.

Oliver Goldsmith

⊢ 1730—1774 *English essayist, poet, novelist and dramatist*

Logicians have but ill defined
As rational the human mind.
Logic, they say, belongs to man,
But let them prove it if they can.

Remy de Gourmont

⊢ 1858—1915 *French novelist*

Man associates ideas not according to logic or verifiable exactitude, but according to his pleasure and interests. It is for this reason that most truths are nothing but prejudices.

Robert Graves

⊢ 1895—1985 *English poet and novelist*

Intuition is the supra-logic that cuts out all the routine processes of thought and leaps straight from the problem to the answer.

The difference between prose, logic and poetic thought is simple. The logician uses words as a builder uses bricks, for the unemotional deadness of his academic prose; and is always coining newer, deader words with a natural preference for Greek formations. The poet avoids the entire vocabulary of logic unless for satiric purposes, and treats words as living creatures with a preference for those with long emotional histories dating from medieval times. Poetry at its purest is, indeed, a defiance of logic. —[81]: Genius

Franz Grillparzer

⊢ 1791—1872 *Austrian playwright and author*

Morality, a muzzle for the will; logic, a climbing iron for the mind. —[82]

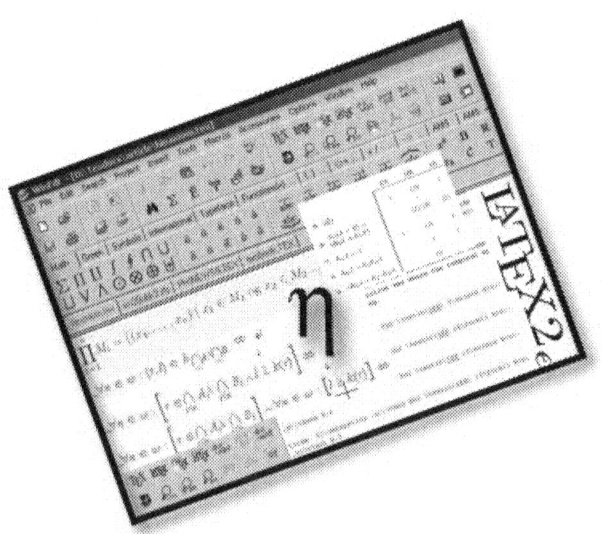

Jim Hankinson

⊢ *American philosopher*

Logic, as a formal study, is fiendishly difficult, and best left well alone. —[83]:38

Suggested by Ilpo Halonen

Richard M. Hare

⊢ 1919— *English philosopher*

Our argument ... will result, not upon logic by itself – though without logic we should never have got to this point – but upon the fortunate contingent fact that people who would take this logically possible view, after they had really imagined themselves in the other man's position, are extremely rare. —[84]: 171

Gilbert Harman

⊢ *American philosopher*

Count as logic only as much as you have to ... —[85]: 79

Suggested by John Symons

William Hazlitt

⊢ 1778—1830 *English essayist*

The most fluent talkers or most plausible reasoners are not always the justest thinkers. —[86]

Suggested by David Makinson

Oliver Heavside

⊢ 1850—1925 *English physicist*

Logic can be patient for it is eternal. —[87]: 3

Suggested by George Englebretsen

Friedrich Hebbel

⊢ 1813—1883 *German-Austrian dramatist*

If language had been the creation not of poetry but of logic, we should only have one.

Georg Wilhelm Friedrich Hegel

⊢ 1770—1831 *German philosopher*

Into all that becomes something inward for men, an image or conception as such, into all that he makes his own, language has penetrated ... logic must certainly be said to be the supernatural element which permeates every relationship of man to nature, his sensation, intuition, desire, need, instinct, and simply by so doing transforms it into something human, even though only formally human, into ideas and purposes. —[89]: 31–32.

Frank Herbert

⊢ 1920—1986 *American science-fiction writer*

Deep in the human unconscious is a pervasive need for a logical universe that makes sense. But the real universe is always one step beyond logic. —[88]

One of the best things to come out of the home computer revolution could be the general and widespread understanding of how severely limited logic really is. —[88]

Alexander Herzen

⊢ 1812—1870 *Russian journalist and political thinker*

You can no more bridle passions with logic than you can justify them in the law courts. Passions are facts and not dogmas. —[93]: vol. 2, pt. 5, ch. 41 (1921)

Jaakko Hintikka

⊢ 1929— *Finish logician and philosopher*

The epistemology of logic, or the logic of epistemology? It's all the same to me! —[90]

Reprinted by the kind permission of Jaakko Hintikka

In mathematics the proof of pudding is its proof. —[91]

Reprinted by the kind permission of Jaakko Hintikka

Alfred Hitchcock

⊢ 1899—1980 *American director*

Logic is boring. —[92]

Suggested by Ilpo Halonen

Thomas Hobbes

⊢ 1588—1679 *English philosopher*

To understand this for sense it is not required that a man should be a geometrician or a logician, but that he should be mad.[1]

[1] 'This' refers to the volume generated by revolving the region under $1/x$ from 1 to infinity has finite volume.

Wilfrid Hodges

⊢ *English logician and mathematician*

Other authors, less coherently, suggested that Cantor had used the wrong positive integers. He should have allowed integers which have infinite decimal expansions to the left, like the p-adic integers. To these people I usually sent the comment that they were quite right, the set of real numbers does have the same cardinality as the set of natural numbers in their sense of natural numbers; but the phrase 'natural number' already has a meaning, and that meaning is not theirs. —[97]

Eric Hoffer

⊢ 1902—1983 *American philosopher*

The Greeks invented logic but were not fooled by it. —[94]

James P. Hogan

⊢ 1941— *American science-fiction writer*

Scientists are the easiest to fool. They think in straight, predictable, directable, and therefore misdirectable, lines. The only world they know is the one where everything has a logical explanation and things are what they appear to be. Children and conjurors—they terrify me. Scientists are no problem; against them I feel quite confident. —[95]

Oliver Wendell Holmes

⊢ 1809—1894 *American author and physician*

Insanity is often the logic of an accurate mind overtasked. —[98]: ch. 2

Logic is logic. That's all I say. —[99]

A page of history is worth a pound of logic. —[99]

Suggested by John Symons

Have you heard of the wonderful one-hoss shay,
That was built in such a logical way
It ran a hundred years to a day. —[99]

Sherlock Holmes

⊢ *English detective*

Crime is common. Logic is rare. —[63]: The Copper Beeches

Suggested by Brian F. Chellas

I cannot agree with those who rank modesty among the virtues. To the logician all things should be seen exactly as they are, and to underestimate one's self is as much a departure from truth as to exaggerate one's own powers. —[63]: The Greek Interpreter

Ah! My dear Watson, there we come into those realms of conjecture, where the most logical mind may be at fault. —[63]: The Adventure of the Empty House

I never guess. It is a shocking habit destructive to the logical faculty. —[63]: The Sign of Four, ch. 1

From a drop of water a logician could predict an Atlantic or a Niagara. —[61]

It is a capital mistake to theorize before one has data. —[62]

Suggested by David Makinson

... it is not really difficult to construct a series of inferences, each dependent upon its predecessor and each simple in itself. If, after doing so, one simply knocks out all the central inferences and presents one's audience with the starting-point and the conclusion, one may produce a startling, though possibly a meretricious, effect. —[63]: The Adventure of the Dancing Men

Some facts should be suppressed, or at least, a just sense of proportion should be observed in treating them. The only point in the case which deserved mention was the curious analytical reasoning from effects to causes, by which I succeeded in unravelling it. —[63]: The Sign of Four, ch. 1

How often have I said to you that when you have eliminated the impossible, whatever remains, *however improbable*, must be the truth? —[63]: The Sign of Four

Suggested by David Makinson

Like all other arts, the science of deduction and analysis is one which can only be acquired by long and patient study, nor is life long enough to allow any mortal to attain the highest possible perfection in it. Before turning to those moral and mental aspects of the matter which present the greatest difficulties, let the inquirer begin by mastering more elementary problems. —[61]

All knowledge comes useful to the detective. —[63]: The Valley of Fear

When a fact appears opposed to a long train of deductions it invariably proves to be capable of bearing some other interpretation. —[61]

Suggested by David Makinson

Elbert Hubbard

⊢ 1856—1915 *American author*

Logic is one thing and commonsense another. —[100]

Victor Hugo

⊢ 1802—1885 *French dramatist, poet and writer*

Freedom in art, freedom in society, this is the double goal towards which all consistent and logical minds must strive. —[101]

Suggested by Joao Marcos

Human League

⊢ *British pop-band*

I believe in truth, so I lie a lot. —[102]

Julian Huxley

⊢ 1887—1975 *English biologist*

... it is curiosity, initiative, originality, and the ruthless application of honesty that count in research—much more than feats of logic and memory alone.

Thomas H. Huxley

⊢ 1825—1895 *English biologist*

Science is simply commonsense at its best, that is, rigidly accurate in observation, and merciless to fallacy in logic.

Logical consequences are the scarecrows of fools and the beacons of wise men. —[103]

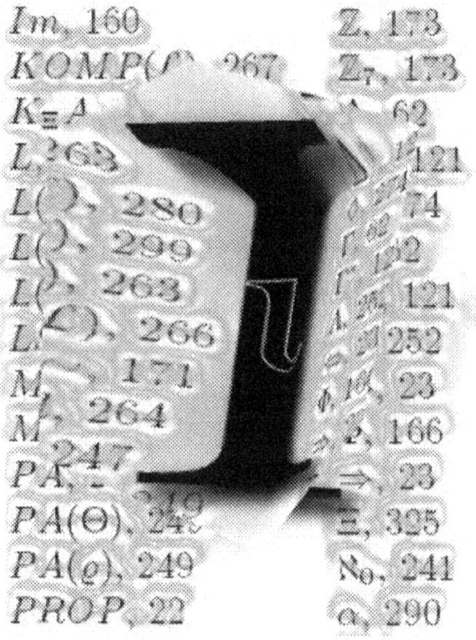

Robert Green Ingersoll

⊢ 1833—1899 *American writer*

Insolence is not logic; epithets are the arguments of malice.

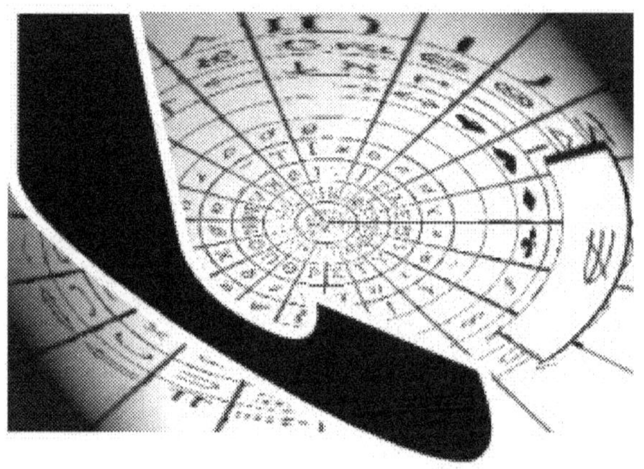

Carl Gustav Jacob Jacobi

⊢ 1915—1994 *German mathematician*

One should always generalize.

Mathematics is the science of what is clear by itself.

William James

⊢ 1842—1910 *American philosopher*

The union of the mathematician with the poet, fervor with measure, passion with correctness, this surely is the ideal.

Samuel Johnson

⊢ 1709—1784 *English author, critic and lexicographer*

Sir, I have found you an argument. I am not obliged to find you an understanding.

Raymond F. Jones

⊢ 1915—1994 *American science-fiction writer*

Logic hasn't wholly dispelled the society of witches and prophets and sorcerers and soothsayers. —[105]

Joseph Joubert

⊢ 1754—1824 *French moralist*

Logic works, metaphysics contemplates.

Journal of Applied Non-Classical Logics

⊢ *Logic journal*

Maybe, if it were yesterday, I could fly, or possibly not [— said Tweety]. —[104]

Suggested by Joao Marcos

Benjamin Jowett

⊢ 1817—1893 *English educator and Greek scholar*

Logic is neither a science nor an art, but a dodge.

Immanuel Kant

⊢ 1724—1804 *German philosopher*

Human knowledge is a process of approximation. In the focus of experience, there is comparative clarity. But the discrimination of this clarity leads into the penumbral background. There are always questions left over. The problem is to discriminate exactly what we know vaguely. —[106]: Logic

Suggested by John Sowa

If we only knew what we know ... we would be astonished by the treasures contained in our knowledge. —[51]

Suggested by John Sowa

Thoughts without content are empty, intuitions without concepts are blind. —[107]: Transcendental Logic, Introduction, part 1, p. 57

John Keats

⊢ 1795—1821 *English poet*

I have never yet been able to perceive how anything can be known for truth by consecutive reasoning—and yet it must be. —[108]: To Benjamin Bailey, November 22, 1817

Suggested by David Makinson

Johannes Kepler

⊢ 1571—1630 *German astronomer*

A mind is accustomed to mathematical deduction, when confronted with the faulty foundations of astrology, resists a long, long time, like an obstinate mule, until compelled by beating and curses to put its foot into that dirty puddle.

Omar Khayyám

⊢ 11th—12th century *Persian astrnomer and poet*

The Grape that can with Logic absolute
The Two-and-Seventy jarring Sects confute. —[109]: st. 43

Lord Kelvin (William Thompson)

⊢ 1824—1907 *English physicist*

Better a rough answer to the right question than an exact answer to the wrong one.

Suggested by John Sowa

Stephen C. Kleene

⊢ 1909—1994 *American logician and mathematician*

It will be very important as we proceed to keep in mind this distinction between the logic we are studying (the object logic) and our use of logic in studying it (the observers logic). To any student who is not ready to do so, we suggest that he close the book now, and pick some other subject instead, such as acrostics or beekeeping. —[110]: 3

Suggested by Jørgen Villadsen

Daniel Kolak

⊢ 1955— *Croatian-American philosopher*

What does logic have to do with *neuro*logy, you ask? I'll tell you. From the computational standpoint, the brain is hardware, theories are software, but logic is the operating system. Not the logic we study: that's a formal language. The logic that runs us is what I call *noumenal logic.* It's what the brain and the cosmos have in common. The Greeks called it *logos.* —[111]

Reprinted by the kind permission of Daniel Kolak

Geometry: the shape of empty space. Probability: the pattern of no pattern. Logic: the way of no way. Understanding the *necessary* structure of nothingness is the algebra, the key to the eventual reunification of mathematics, science and philosophy. The Unholy Trinity. —[111]

Reprinted by the kind permission of Daniel Kolak

Leopold Kronecker

⊢ 1823—1891 *German mathematician*

God made the integers, all else is the work of man. —[112]

Number theorists are like lotus-eaters—having once tasted of this food they can never give it up. —[113]

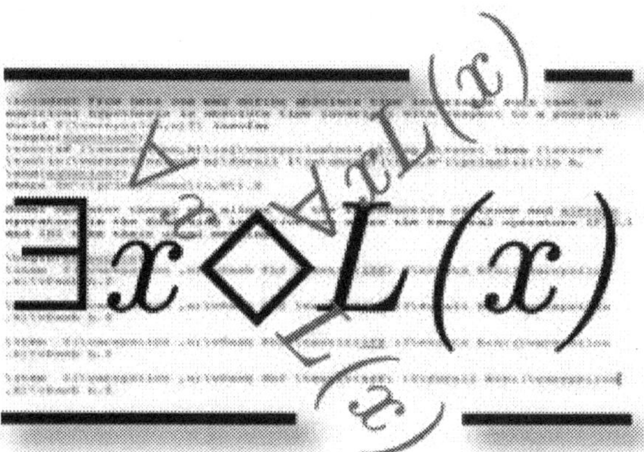

Pierre-Simon Laplace

⊢ 1749—1827 *French mathematician*

Such is the advantage of a well-constructed language that its simplified notation often becomes the source of profound theories.

Suggested by Joao Marcos

It is remarkable that a science which began with the consideration of games of chance should have become the most important object of human knowledge.

Muhammad Legenhausen

⊢ *Iranian logician*

Modal Logic Blues

(Chorus:)
Modal Logic Blues, Modal Logic Blues,
It just might be you're gonna possibly do,
Yeah, I believe that it's necessarily true.
Modal logic is for modal situations;
Modal logic has got modal implications.
Every world with you or me, we've got a good relation,
Cause it's **S5** and we've got the Barcan formulation!

Chorus

Modal logic ain't really nothin' new,
Just a quasi-intension, a funky function or two.
Maybe you read about the sea battle in days of yore.
Well, it's the same old story but we're talkin' 'bout atomic war.

Chorus

Gottfried Wilhelm Friedrich Leibniz

⊢ 1646—1716 *German philosopher*

By relieving the brain of all unnecessary work, a good notation sets it free to concentrate on more advanced problems, and in effect increases the mental power of the race. Before the introduction of the Arabic notation, multiplication was difficult, and the division even of integers called into play the highest mathematical faculties ... . Civilization advances by extending the number of important operations which we can perform without thinking about them. —[114]: The Art of Discovery

Suggested by John Sowa

Stanislaw Lesniewski

⊢ 1886—1939 *Polish logician and mathematician*

Logic is a formal exposition of intuition. —[173]

Suggested by Jan Wolenski

Georg Christoph Lichtenberg

⊢ 1742—1799 *German physicist, astronomer and mathematician*

I have often noticed that when people come to understand a mathematical proposition in some other way than that of the ordinary demonstration, they promptly say, 'Oh, I see. That's how it must be.' This is a sign that they explain it to themselves from within their own system.

Don de Lillo

⊢ 1936— *American writer*

One way of viewing mathematics is in terms of number. I guess you know what the other way is. I'll say the word in a more expressive language so there'll be no doubt.

I wish you wouldn't.

Logik, softly said. —[115]: 272

Suggested by George Englebretsen

John Locke

⊢ 1632—1704 *English philosopher*

Logic is the anatomy of thought.

Thus learned ignorance, and this art of keeping even inquisitive men from true knowledge, hath been propagated in the world, and hath much perplexed, whilst it pretended to inform the understanding. For we see that other well-meaning and wise men, whose education and parts had not acquired that acuteness, could intelligibly express themselves to one another; and in its plain use make a benefit of language. But though unlearned men well enough understood the words white and black, and had constant notions of the ideas signified by those words; yet there were philosophers found who had learning and subtlety enough to prove that snow was black; i.e. to prove that white was black. Whereby they had the advantage to destroy the instruments and means of discourse, conversation, instruction, and society; whilst, with great art and subtlety, they did no more but perplex and confound the signification of words, and thereby render language less useful than the real defects of it had made it; a gift which the illiterate had not attained to. —[116]: Book III, X – Of the Abuse of Words

Suggested by Joao Marcos

James Lowell

⊢ 1819—1891 *American romantic poet*

It ['The Ancient Mariner'] is marvellous in its mastery over that delightfully fortuitous inconsequence that is the adamantine logic of dreamland.

Jan Łukasiewicz

⊢ 1878—1956 *Polish logician*

Logic is the moral of speech and thought. —[173]

Suggested by Jan Wolenski

Lord Mansfield (William Murray)

⊢ 1705—1793 *Earl of Mansfield*

Consider what you think justice requires, and decide accordingly. But never give your reasons; for your judgement will probably be right, but your reasons will certainly be wrong. —[36]

Suggested by David Makinson

Imelda Marcos

⊢ 1929— *Philippine lady*

I am beyond logic and rationality.

Thomas B. Macaulay

⊢ 1800—1859 *English historian and awyer*

The knowledge of the theory of logic has no tendency whatever to make men good reasoners.

Logicians may reason about abstractions. But the great mass of men must have images. The strong tendency of the multitude in all ages and nations to idolatry can be explained on no other principle.

Karl Marx

⊢ 1818—1883 *German revolutionary*

Logic is the currency of the mind.

Suggested by Johan van Benthem

Maarten Marx

⊢ 1964— *Dutch logician*

The dynamic definition in relation algebraic terms almost shows the two parents in action producing their offspring. —[117]: 697

Suggested by Patrick Blackburn

Reprinted by the kind permission of Maarten Marx

John McCarthy

⊢ 1927— *American logician and computer scientist*

Maybe physics is inexhaustible, but maybe it isn't. Here's why it might not be. Consider the Life World based on Conway's Life cellular automaton. It has been shown that self-reproducing universal computers are possible as configurations in the Life World. Therefore, one could have physicists in the Life World, but their physics would not be inexhaustible. They could discover or at least conjecture that their fundamental physics was a particular cellular automaton. However, their mathematics could be the same as ours—and therefore inexhaustible.
—[118]: May 15, 2004

Herman Melville

⊢ 1819—1891 *American author*

The strong arm, my lord, is no argument, though it overcomes all logic. —[119]: vol. 3, ch. 104

H.L. Mencken

⊢ 1880—1956 *American editor and author*

The psychologists and the metaphysicians wrangle endlessly over the nature of the thinking process in man, but no matter how violently they differ otherwise they all agree that it has little to do with logic and is not much conditioned by overt facts.

... logic, the refuge of fools. The pedant and the priest have always been the most expert of logicians and the most diligent disseminators of nonsense and worse. —[120]: 75

Faith may be defined briefly as an illogical belief in the occurrence of the improbable.

Metrodorus of Chios

⊢ ca 400 BC *Greek philosopher*

None of us knows anything, not even whether we know or do not know, nor do we know whether not knowing and knowing exist, nor in general whether there is anything or not.

Ceslaw Milosz

⊢ 1911—2004 *Polish writer*

Grow your tree of falsehood from a small grain of truth. Do not follow those who lie in contempt of reality. Let your lie be even more logical than the truth itself, so the weary travelers may find repose.

John Milton

⊢ 1608—1674 *English poet*

Reason also is choice. —[121]

Chaos umpire sits
And by decision more
embroils the fray
by which he reigns: next
him high arbiter
Chance governs all. —[121]

William Minto

⊢ 1845—1893 *Scottish logician and literary critic*

An attitude of philosophic doubt, of suspended judgement, is repugnant to the natural man. Belief is an independent joy to him. —[122]: Introduction

Maria Mitchell

⊢ 1818—1889 *American astronomer*

We especially need imagination in science. It is not all mathematics, nor all logic, but it is somewhat beauty and poetry.

Richard Mitchell

⊢ 1935—2002 *American writer*

Thought control, like birth control, is best undertaken as long as possible before the fact. Many grown-ups will obstinately persist, if only now and then, in composing small strings of sentences in their heads and achieving at least momentary logic. This probably cannot be prevented, but we have learned how to minimize the consequences by arranging that such grown-ups will be unable to pursue that logic very far. If they were at home in the technology of writing, there's no telling how much social disorder they would cause by thinking things out at length. Our schools have chosen to cut this danger off as close to the root as possible, thus taking measures to preclude not only the birth of thought but its conception. They give the pill to even the youngest children, but just to be on the safe side, they give it to everybody else, too, especially all would-be schoolteachers. —[123]

Michel de Montaigne

⊢ 1533—1592 *French philosopher and writer*

Everyone may speak truly, but to speak logically, prudently, and adequately is a talent few possess. —[124]: I, 9

If, like the truth, falsehood had only one face, we should know better where we are, for we should then take the opposite of what a liar said to be the truth. But the opposite of the truth has a hundred thousand shapes and a limitless field. —[124]: I, 31

Augustus de Morgan

⊢ 1806—1871 *English mathematician and logician*

Every science that has thriven has thriven upon its own symbols: logic, the only science which is admitted to have made no improvements in century after century, is the only one which has grown no symbols. —[125]: 184

I end with a word on the new symbols which I have employed. Most writers on logic strongly object to all symbols ... I should advise the reader not to make up his mind on this point until he has well weighed two facts which nobody disputes, both separately and in connexion. First, logic is the only science which has made no progress since the revival of letters; secondly, logic is the only science which has produced no growth of symbols. —[125]: 185

Mother Teresa

⊢ 1910—1997 *Indian Nobel Price lauterate*

People are unreasonable, illogical, and self-centered. Love them anyway.

Cardinal Newman

⊢ 1801—1890 *English cardinal*

I recollect an acquaintance saying to me that 'the Oriel Common Room stank of Logic.'—[126]

Suggested by David Makinson

Nicholas of Cusa

⊢ 1401—1464 *German cardinal and mathematician*

All we know of the truth is that the absolute truth, such as it is, is beyond our reach. —[127]

Friedrich Nietzsche

⊢ 1844—1900 *German philosopher*

Logic, too, also rests on assumptions that do not correspond to anything in the real world, e.g., on the assumption that there are equal things, that the same thing is identical at different points in time: But this science arose as a result of the opposite belief (that such things actually exist in the real world). And it is the same with mathematics, which would certainly never have arisen if it had been understood from the beginning that there is no such thing in nature as a perfectly straight line, a true circle, and absolute measure. —[128]: On First and Last Things, section 11

Andrea Nye

⊢ *American philosopher*

Logic in its final perfection is insane. —[129]: 171

Suggested by Ilpo Halonen

Logic, one current argument goes, is the creation of defensive male subjects who have lost touch with their lived experience and define all being in rigid oppositional categories modeled on a primal contrast between male and female. —[129]: 4

Suggested by Ilpo Halonen

Logic celebrates the unity of a pathological masculine self-identity that cannot listen and recognizes only negation and not difference. —[129]: 5

Suggested by Ilpo Halonen

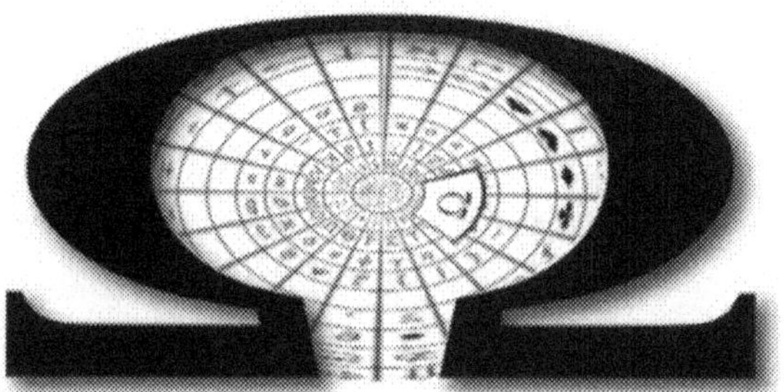

C.O. Oakley

⊢ *American mathematician*

The study of mathematics cannot be replaced by any other activity that will train and develop man's purely logical faculties to the same level of rationality. —[130]

Emmuska, Baroness Orczy

⊢ 1865—1947 *English author and playwright*

This, mayhap, was not logic, but it was something more potent, more real than logic—the soft insinuating voice of Sentiment. —[131]: bk. 2, ch. 5

Jane O'Reilly

⊢ *American humorist*

Logic and hope fade somewhat by thirty-six, when endings seem more like clear warnings than useful experience. —[132]

Oxford University

⊢ *English university*

14th century rule of Oxford University:
Bachelors and Masters of Art who do not follow Aristotle's philosophy are subject to a fine of 5 shillings for each point of divergence. —[14]: 205

Suggested by George Englebretsen

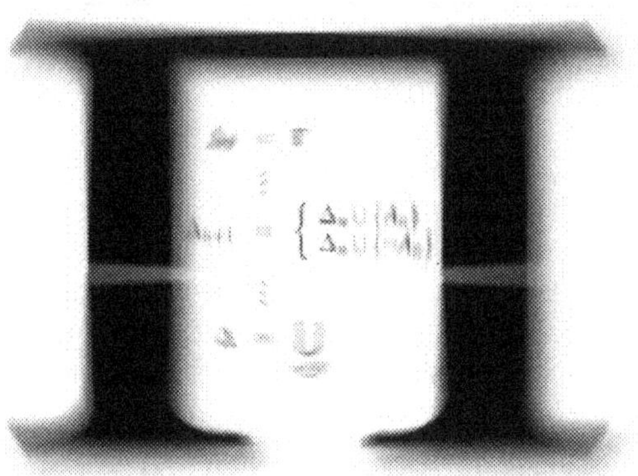

Blaise Pascal

⊢ 1623—1662 *French scientist and philosopher*

The heart has arguments with which the logic of mind is not acquainted. —[133]

There are two types of mind ... the mathematical, and what might be called the intuitive. The former arrives at its views slowly, but they are firm and rigid; the latter is endowed with greater flexibility and applies itself simultaneously to the diverse lovable parts of that which it loves. —[133]

Charles S. Peirce

⊢ 1839—1914 *American philosopher*

Find a scientific man who proposes to get along without any metaphysics ... and you have found one whose doctrines are thoroughly vitiated by the crude and uncriticized metaphysics with which they are packed. —[134]: 1.129

Suggested by John Sowa

The opinion which is fated to be ultimately agreed to by all who investigate is what we mean by truth. —[134]: 5.407

Suggested by John Sowa

Truth, what can this possibly mean except it be that there is one destined upshot to inquiry with reference to the question in hand. —[134]: 3.432

Suggested by John Sowa

Truth is that concordance of an abstract statement with the ideal limit towards which endless investigation would tend to bring scientific belief, which concordance the abstract statement may possess by virtue of the confession of its inaccuracy and one-sidedness, and this confession is an essential ingredient of truth. —[134]: 5.565

Suggested by John Sowa

That truth is the correspondence of a representation with its object is, as Kant says [1787, A58, B82], merely the nominal definition of it. Truth belongs exclusively to propositions. A proposition has a subject (or set of subjects) and a predicate. The subject is a sign; the predicate is a sign; and the proposition is a sign that the predicate is a sign of that of which the subject is a sign. If it be so, it is true. But what does this correspondence, or reference of the sign to its object, consist in? The pragmaticist answers this question as follows [...] if we can find out the right method of thinking and can follow it out, the right method of transforming signs, then truth can be nothing more nor less than the last result to which the following out of this method would ultimately carry us. —[134]: EP 2.379–380

Suggested by John Sowa

... it is a most elementary point without a perfectly clear understanding of which it is impossible to take one step in logic without danger of setting your foot into mud. My proposition is that logic, in the strict sense of the term, has nothing to do with how you think. —[135]: 143

Suggested by Dag Westerstahl

Alan J. Perlis

⊢ 1922—1990 *American computer scientist*

A year spent in artificial intelligence is enough to make one believe in God. —[136]

Suggested by John Sowa

Laurence J. Peter

⊢ 1919—1988 *Canadian educator and writer*

Against logic there is no armor like ignorance. —[137]

A man doesn't know what he knows until he knows what he doesn't know. —[137]

Kenneth L. Pike

⊢ 1912—2000 *American linguist*

Logic may be viewed, perhaps, as a machine which is designed, at best, to be such that when we feed into it certain data and turn the logic crank, we inevitably get certain conclusions out the other end. Logic is designed to give inevitably true results starting from known true – or assumed-to-be-true – premises. Logic is a wonderful tool when we want only logical conclusions. We should not reject such a machine merely because it is not equipped to handle all of reality. The scientist who commits himself to use a logic machine is doing wisely, qua scientist, for use on data of science. But if he feeds into that machine convictions that there is no God, or ignores God because He is not in his corpus of data, and then draws from his logic the conclusion that God does not exist, his conclusion is irrelevant. Logic is a tool; it should not be made into a religion. —[138]

Pontius Pilate

⊢ —36 *Governor of the Roman province of Judaea*

Veritas? Quid est veritas? —[139]

Suggested by Joao Marcos

Luigi Pirandello

⊢ 1867—1936 *Italian playwright*

Logic is one thing, the human animal another. You can quite easily propose a logical solution to something and at the same time hope in your heart of hearts it won't work out. —[140]

Henri Poincare

⊢ 1854—1912 *French mathematician*

Thus, be it understood, to demonstrate a theorem, it is neither necessary nor even advantageous to know what it means. The geometer might be replaced by the 'logic piano' imagined by Stanley Jevons; or, if you choose, a machine might be imagined where the assumptions were put in at one end, while the theorems came out at the other, like the legendary Chicago machine where the pigs go in alive and come out transformed into hams and sausages. No more than these machines need the mathematician know what he does.

It is by logic that we prove, but by intuition that we discover.

Port Royal Logic

Logic: The art of using reason well in the acquisition of the knowledge of things, both for one's own instruction and that of others. —[141]

Winthrop Mackworth Praed

⊢ 1802—1839 *English poet*

Of science and logic he chatters,
As fine and as fast as he can;
Though I am no judge of such matters,
I'm sure he's a talented man. —[142]: The Talented Man

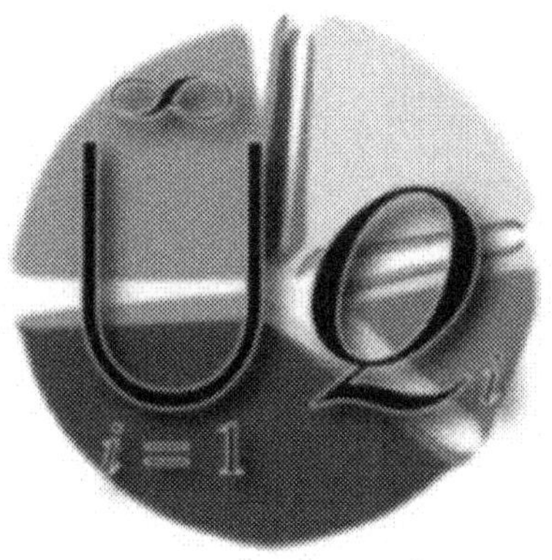

W.V. Quine

⊢ 1908—2000 *American philosopher*

Logic chases truth up the tree of grammar. —[143]

Reprinted by the kind permission of Douglas B. Quine

One man's antinomy is another man's falsidical paradox, give or take a couple of thousand years. —[144]: 9

Suggested by Joao Marcos

Reprinted by the kind permission of Douglas B. Quine

If pressed to supplement Tweedledee's ostensive definition of logic with a discursive definition of the same subject, I would say that logic is the systematic study of the logical truths. Pressed further, I would say that a sentence is logically true if all sentences with its grammatical structure are true. Pressed further still, I would say to read this book. —[143]

Ayn Rand

⊢ 1896—1982 *Russian-American philosopher*

There are only two means by which men can deal with one another: guns or logic. Force or persuasion. Those who know that they cannot win by means of logic, have always resorted to guns. —[146]

Suggested by Joao Marcos

Contradictions do not exist. Whenever you think that you are facing a contradiction, check your premises. You will find that one of them is wrong. —[145]

Georg Friedrich Bernhard Riemann

⊢ 1826—1866 *German mathematician*

If only I had the theorems! Then I should find the proofs easily enough.

Philip Robinson

⊢ 1735—1815

And when the future hinges
on the next words that are said,
Don't let logic interfere,
believe your heart instead.

Rodan of Alexandria

⊢ *Biblical figure*

Only a brave person is willing to honestly admit, and fearlessly to face, what a sincere and logical mind discovers.

Donald Rumsfeld

⊢ 1932— *21st American secretary of defence*

Reports that say that something hasn't happened are always interesting to me, because as we know, there are known knowns; there are things we know we know. We also know there are known unknowns; that is to say we know there are some things we do not know. But there are also unknown unknowns, the ones we don't know we don't know. —[147]

Suggested by David Makinson

There's another way to phrase that and that is that the absence of evidence is not the evidence of absence. It is basically saying the same thing in a different way. Simply because you do not have evidence that something does exist does not mean that you have evidence that it doesn't exist. —[147]

I believe what I said yesterday. I don't know what I said, but I know what I think, and, well, I assume it's what I said. —[147]

Well, um, you know, something's neither good nor bad but thinking makes it so, I suppose, as Shakespeare said. —[147]

If I know the answer I'll tell you the answer, and if I don't, I'll just respond, cleverly. —[147]

Bertrand Russell

⊢ 1872—1970 *English logician and philosopher*

Logic is hell! —[188]: 63

Suggested by Ilpo Halonen

The true function of logic, ... as applied to matters of experience, ... is analytic rather than constructive; taken a priori, it shows the possibility of hitherto unsuspected alternatives more often than the impossibility of alternatives which seemed prima facie possible. Thus, while it liberates imagination as to what the world may be, it refuses to legislate as to what the world *is*. —[149]

The conception of the necessary unit of all that is resolves itself into the poverty of the imagination, and a freer logic emancipates us from the straitwaistcoated benevolent institution which idealism palms off as the totality of being. —[149]

In fact the opposition of instinct and reason is mainly illusory. Instinct, intuition, or insight is what first leads to the beliefs which subsequent reason confirms or confutes; but the confirmation, where it is possible, consists, in the last analysis, of agreement with other beliefs no less instinctive. Reason is a harmonizing, controlling force rather than a creative one. Even in the most purely logical realms, it is insight that first arrives at what is new. —[149]

Thus [pure] mathematics may be defined as the subject in which we never know what we are talking about, nor whether what we are saying is true. —[150]

Man is a rational animal—so at least I have been told. Throughout a long life, I have looked diligently for evidence in favor of this statement, but so far I have not had the good fortune to come across it, though I have searched in many countries spread over three continents. —[148]: An Outline of Intellectual Rubbish

In a man whose reasoning powers are good, fallacious arguments are evidence of bias. —[148]

George Santayana

⊢ 1863—1952 *American philosopher*

The lover knows much more about absolute good and universal beauty than any logician or theologian, unless the latter, too, be lovers in disguise.

It is possible to be a master in false philosophy—easier, in fact, than to be a master in the truth, because a false philosophy can be made as simple and consistent as one pleases. —[151]: ch. 1

Suggested by Joao Marcos

Friedrich Von Schlegel

⊢ 1772—1892 *German philosopher*

Only through religion can logic develop into philosophy, only from this source stems that which makes philosophy more than science. And without religion we will have only novels, or the triviality today called belles lettres instead of an eternally rich and infinite poetry. —[152]: Idea 11

Mathematics is, as it were, a sensuous logic, and relates to philosophy as do the arts, music, and plastic art to poetry. —[152]: Aphorism 365

Dana Scott

⊢ *American mathematician and logician*

Here is what I consider one of the biggest mistakes of all in modal logic: concentration on a system with just one modal operator. The only way to have any philosophically significant results in deontic logic or epistemic logic is to combine these operators with: Tense operators (otherwise how can you formulate principles of change?); the logical operators (otherwise how can you compare the relative with the absolute?); the operators like historical or physical necessity (otherwise how can you relate the agent to his environment?); and so on and so on. —[153]: 143

Gaius Plinius Secundus

⊢ 23—79 *Roman naturalist*

This only is certain, that there is nothing certain; and nothing more miserable and yet more arrogant than man.

William Shakespeare

⊢ 1564—1616 *English dramatist and poet*

Though this be madness, yet there is method in't. —[154]: Hamlet, act 2, sc. 2, l. 206–7.[1]

There is a river in Macedon, and there is moreover a river in Monmouth. It is called Wye at Monmouth, but it is out of my prains what is the name of the other river; but tis all one, tis alike as my fingers is to my fingers, and there is salmons in both. —[154]: Henry V, act 4, sc. 7, l. 26–31.[2]

Good reasons must, of force, give place to better. —[154]: Julius Ceasar

Suggested by David Makinson

[1] Referring to the logic in Hamlet's mad and weird discourse. The expression, there is 'method in my/his/her madness' has entered common usage.

[2] Fluellen's logic is as quaint as his language when he proves that Henry V is as great a soldier as Alexander the Great.

George Bernard Shaw

⊢ 1856—1950 *Irish dramatist*

The American Constitution, one of the few modern political documents drawn up by men who were forced by the sternest circumstances to think out what they really had to face, instead of chopping logic in a university classroom. —[155]

Consistency is the enemy of enterprise, just as symmetry is the enemy of art. —[156]

Censorship ends in logical completeness when nobody is allowed to read any books except the books nobody reads. —[156]

The reasonable man adapts himself to the world; the unreasonable man persists in trying to adapt the world to himself. Therefore all progress depends on the unreasonable man. —[156]

The man who listens to Reason is lost : Reason enslaves all whose minds are not strong enough to master her. —[156]: Maxims for Revolutionist

Suggested by David Makinson

Frank Sinatra

⊢ 1915—1998 *American singer and entertainer*

Fear is the enemy of logic. There is no more debilitating, crushing, self-defeating, sickening thing in the world—to an individual or to a nation.

Raymond M. Smullyan

⊢ 1919— *American logician, magician, musician and essayist*

Only an idiot would believe this sentence. —[160]

Unamuno gives reasons why reasons are bad. And the reasons he gives are incredibly bad! —[159]

A young man who was both extremely sensitive and intelligent, worked out a logical proof showing that the most rational thing he could do was commit suicide. The proof was long and involved, but the conclusion was quite definite. He should commit suicide. And so he thought of what would be the most pleasant way of doing so. At first he thought that the most pleasant way would be an overdose of opium, but then he thought, 'Just because opium is pleasant in non-lethal doses, it doesn't follow that a lethal dose of opium is pleasant. For all we know, a lethal dose might be quite painful!' And so, he hit on the following ingenious plan: He would take a non-lethal dose of opium, enough to put him to sleep for several hours. He had a gun timed to shoot him in his sleep after 2 hours. He set the time machine and took the drug. After falling asleep, he realized to his horror that he didn't have any pleasant dreams as he had expected, but was simply cut off from the outer world and that his mind worked with perfect clarity, as if he were lying in a quite room with his eyes closed. What horrified him was the thought of the boring next two hours he had to spend. [Of course, there was no way he could wake himself up.] He then ruminated over the whole situation, congratulated himself on his 'rationality' and to give himself something to do, he reviewed his proof that he should commit suicide. To his horror, he discovered a mistake! —[158]

Suggested by Joao Marcos

A member of a 'joke-makers' club' invited a friend to one of their banquets. At the banquet, the friend was quite puzzled by the goings on—every now and then, someone would arise, call out a number and everyone else would laugh. When the friend asked what was going on, the host replied: 'We joke-makers don't want to take the time to tell the whole joke, so we assign a number to each joke, and when the number of a joke is called, it calls to mind the joke, and we then laugh.'

First ending: The friend asks the host if he can try it, and the host assents. The friend rises, calls out a number, but no one laughs. When the friend asks the host why no one laughed, the host replied, 'Some people can tell a joke and some cannot!'

Second ending: A man gets up and calls out a very high number, everyone laughs and this one person keeps laughing much longer than everyone else. When the friend asked the host why that man was still laughing, the host replied: 'He hasn't heard that one before.' —[158]: The Philosopher's Dream (the Universal Refutation to all Doctrines)

Suggested by Joao Marcos

Susan Sontag

⊢ 1933— *American writer*

Victims suggest innocence. And innocence, by the inexorable logic that governs all relational terms, suggests guilt. —[161]

Spock (Star Trek)

⊢ *Science-fiction film character*

Logic is the beginning of wisdom, not the end.

Elizabeth Cady Stanton

⊢ 1815—1902 *American author and social reformer*

Human beings lose their logic in their vindictiveness. —[162]

John Steinbeck

⊢ 1902—1968 *American writer*

I know three things will never be believed—the true, the probable, and the logical. —[163]: ch. 2

Supertramp

⊢ *American rock-band*

When I was young, it seemed that life was so wonderful,
a miracle, oh it was beautiful, magical.
And all the birds in the trees, well they'd be singing so happily,
joyfully, playfully watching me.
But then they send me away to teach me how to be
sensible, logical, responsible, practical.
And they showed me a world where I could be
so dependable, clinical, intellectual, cynical.
—[164]: The Logical Song

Lyrics by Roger Hodgson

Suggested by Ilpo Halonen

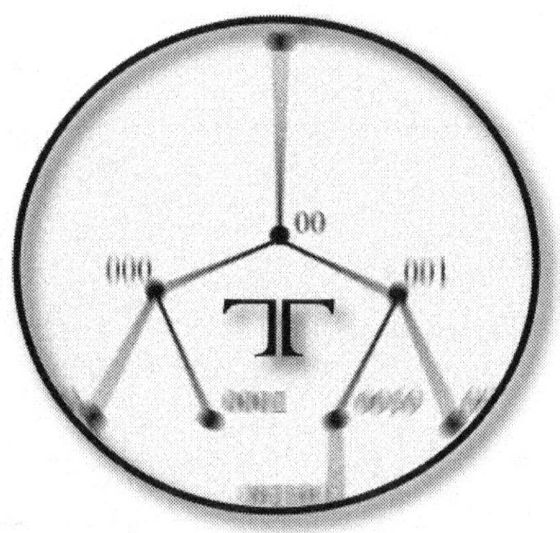

Rabindranath Tagore

⊢ 1861—1941 *Indian writer*

In a mind all logic is like a knife blade. It makes the hand bleed that uses it. —[165]

Talking Heads

⊢ *American rock-band*

Stop Making Sense. —[166]

Suggested by Johan van Benthem

Alfred Tarski

⊢ 1902—1983 *Polish logician*

Logic brings people together, but religion divides them. —[173]

Suggested by Jan Wolenski

I believe, nevertheless, that it is inimical to the progress of science to measure the importance of any research exclusively or chiefly in terms of its usefulness and applicability. We know from the history of science that many important results and discoveries have had to wait centuries before they were applied in any field. And, in my opinion, there are also other important factors which cannot be disregarded in determining the value of a scientific work. It seems to me that there is a special domain of very profound and strong human needs related to scientific research, which are similar in many ways to aesthetic and perhaps religious needs. And it also seems to me that the satisfaction of these needs should be considered an important task of research. Hence, I believe, the question of the value of any research cannot be adequately answered without taking into account the intellectual satisfaction which the results of that research bring to those who understand it and care for it. It may be unpopular and out-of-date to say—but I do not think that a scientific result which gives a better understanding of the world and makes it more harmonious in our eyes should be held in lower esteem than, say, an invention which reduces the cost of paving roads, or improves household plumbing. —[167]

Suggested by Joao Marcos

Alfred Lord Tennyson

⊢ 1809—1892 *English poet*

For nothing worthy proving can be proven,
Nor yet disproven: Wherefore thou be wise. —[168]

Suggested by Paolo Di Gusta

Henry David Thoreau

⊢ 1817—1862 *American author*

Some minds are as little logical or argumentative as nature; they can offer no reason or 'guess,' but they exhibit the solemn and incontrovertible fact. If a historical question arises, they cause the tombs to be opened. Their silent and practical logic convinces the reason and the understanding at the same time. Of such sort is always the only pertinent question and the only satisfactory reply. —[170]: A Week on the Concord and Merrimack Rivers (1849), vol. 1: 265

Time Magazine

⊢ *American news magazine*

Lovers of problem-solving, they are apt to play chess at lunch or doodle in algebra over cocktails, speak an esoteric language that some suspect is just their way of mystifying outsiders. Deeply concerned about logic and sensitive to its breakdown in everyday life, they often annoy friends by asking them to rephrase their questions more logically. —[169]

Richard C. Trench

⊢ 1835—1886 *Irish archbishop and writer*

Grammar is the logic of speech, even as logic is the grammar of reason. —[171]: Lecture 1

Ivan Turgenev

⊢ 1818—1883 *Russian novelist and dramatist*

Nature cares nothing for logic, our human logic: she has her own, which we do not recognize and do not acknowledge until we are crushed under its wheel.

Alan Mathison Turing

⊢ 1912—1954 *English computer scientist*

(1943, New York: the Bell Labs Cafeteria)
His high pitched voice already stood out above the general murmur of well-behaved junior executives grooming themselves for promotion within the Bell corporation. Then he was suddenly heard to say: 'No, I'm not interested in developing a powerful brain. All I'm after is just a mediocre brain, something like the President of the American Telephone and Telegraph Company.'
—[96]: 251

Mark Twain

⊢ 1835—1910 *American writer*

Man is the Reasoning Animal. Such is the claim. I think it is open to dispute. Indeed, my experiments have proven to me that he is the Unreasoning Animal ... In truth, man is incurably foolish. Simple things which other animals easily learn, he is incapable of learning. Among my experiments was this. In an hour I taught a cat and a dog to be friends. I put them in a cage. In another hour I taught them to be friends with a rabbit. In the course of two days I was able to add a fox, a goose, a squirrel and some doves. Finally a monkey. They lived together in peace; even affectionately.

Next, in another cage I confined an Irish Catholic from Tipperary, and as soon as he seemed tame I added a Scotch Presbyterian from Aberdeen. Next a Turk from Constantinople; a Greek Christian from Crete; an Armenian; a Methodist from the wilds of Arkansas; a Buddhist from China; a Brahman from Benares. Finally, a Salvation Army Colonel from Wapping. Then I stayed away for two whole days. When I came back to note results, the cage of Higher Animals was all right, but in the other there was but a chaos of gory odds and ends of turbans and fezzes and plaids and bones and flesh—not a specimen left alive. These Reasoning Animals had disagreed on a theological detail and carried the matter to a Higher Court. —[172]: 180–181

... there is something better than logic.
Indeed? What is it?
Fact. —[172]: 74

Suggested by George Englebretsen

What, then, is the true Gospel of consistency? Change. Who is the really consistent man? The man who changes. Since change is the law of his being, he cannot be consistent if he sticks in a rut.

The time to begin writing an article is when you have finished it to your satisfaction. By that time you begin to clearly and logically perceive what it is you really want to say.

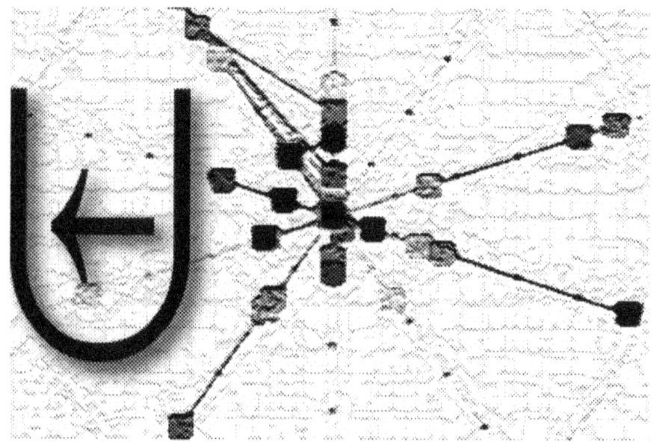

U.S. Ninth Circuit Court of Appeals

We accept the risk that words and ideas have wings we cannot clip and which carry them we know not where. —[176]

22 V

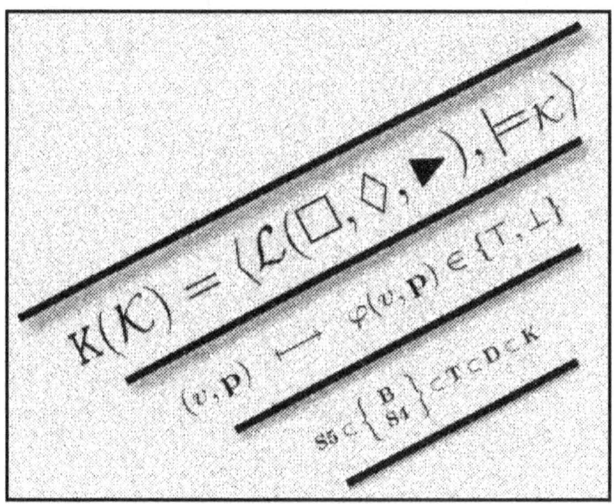

Marquis de Vauvenargues

⊢ 1715—1747 *French writer*

The mind of man is more intuitive than logical, and comprehends more than it can coordinate. —[174]

Suggested by Joao Marcos

Thorstein B. Veblen

⊢ 1857—1929 *American economist*

Invention is the mother of necessity.

The outcome of any serious research can only be to make two questions grow where only one grew before. —[175]

Horace Walpole

⊢ 1717—1797 *English author*

The world is a tragedy to those who feel, but a comedy to those who think.

Andre Weil

⊢ 1906—1998 *French mathematician*

God exists, since Arithmetic is consistent; the Devil exists, since we cannot prove it. —[157]: 257

Suggested by Leo Esakia

Hermann Weyl

⊢ 1885—1955 *German mathematician*

We now come to the decisive step of mathematical abstraction: We forget about what the symbols stand for. The mathematician is concerned with the catalogue alone; he is like the man in the catalogue room who does not care what books or pieces of an intuitively given manifold the symbols of his catalogue denote. He need not be idle; there are many operations which he may carry out with these symbols, without ever having to look at the things they stand for. —[177]

Logic is the hygiene the mathematician practices to keep his ideas healthy and strong. —[178]

Alfred North Whitehead

⊢ 1861—1947 *English mathematician*

Systems, scientific and philosophic, come and go. Each method of limited understanding is at length exhausted. In its prime each system is a triumphant success: In its decay it is an obstructive nuisance.—[180]

Suggested by John Sowa

The conjunction of premises, from which logic proceeds, presupposes that no difficulty will arise from the conjunction of the various unexpressed presuppositions involved in those premises. Both in science and in logic, you have only to develop your argument sufficiently, and sooner or later you are bound to arrive at a contradiction, either internally within the argument, or externally in its reference to fact. —[181]: 14

Suggested by John Sowa

It should be noticed that logical proof starts from premises, and that premises are based upon evidence. Thus evidence is presupposed by logic; at least, it is presupposed by the assumption that logic has any importance. —[181]: 67

Suggested by John Sowa

The premises are conceived in the simplicity of their individual isolation. But there can be no logical test for the possibility that deductive procedure, leading to the elaboration of compositions, may introduce into relevance considerations from which the primitive notions of the topic have been abstracted ... Thus deductive logic has not the coercive supremacy which is conventionally conceded to it. When applied to concrete instances, it is a tentative procedure, finally to be judged by the self-evidence of its issues. —[181]: 144

Suggested by John Sowa

The topic of every science is an abstraction from the full concrete happenings of nature. But every abstraction neglects the influx of the factors omitted into the factors retained. —[181]: 196

Suggested by John Sowa

The only way to rectify our reasonings is to make them as tangible as those of the Mathematicians, so that we can find our error at a glance, and when there are disputes among persons, we can simply say: Let us calculate, without further ado, in order to see who is right. —[182]

Suggested by John Sowa

The task of classifying all the words of language, or what's the same thing, all the ideas that seek expression, is the most stupendous of logical tasks. Anybody but the most accomplished logician must break down in it utterly; and even for the strongest man, it is the severest possible tax on the logical equipment and faculty. —[183]

Suggested by John Sowa

In formal logic, a contradiction is the signal of defeat: but in the evolution of real knowledge, it marks the first step in progress toward victory.

Mathematics in its widest signification is the development of all types of formal, necessary, deductive reasoning. —[179]: Preface

Suggested by Joao Marcos

The ideal of mathematics should be to erect a calculus to facilitate reasoning in connection with every province of thought, or of external experience, in which the succession of thoughts, or of events can be definitively ascertained and precisely stated. So that all serious thought which is not philosophy, or inductive reasoning, or imaginative literature, shall be mathematics developed by means of a calculus. —[179]: Preface

Suggested by Joao Marcos

Walt Whitman

⊢ 1819—1892 *American poet*

Do I contradict myself? Very well then I contradict myself, (I am large, I contain multitudes). —[184]

Suggested by David Makinson

Logic and sermons never convince,
The damp of the night drives deeper into my soul.
(Only what proves itself to every man and woman is so,
Only what nobody denies is so.) —[184]: Section 30

Suggested by Joao Marcos

Jerome Wiesner

⊢ 1915—1994 *13th President of MIT*

Some problems are just too complicated for rational, logical solutions. They admit of insights, not answers.

Oscar Wilde

⊢ 1854—1900 *Irish novelist and poet*

Consistency is the last resort of the unimaginative.

Man is a rational animal who always loses his temper when he is called upon to act in accordance with the dictates of reason.

George F. Will

⊢ *American writer*

The reformers; preferred metaphor is 'leveling the playing field.' They should listen to the logic of their language; fields are leveled by bulldozers. —[185]

John Wilmot

⊢ 1647—1680 *Earl of Rochester*

Reason, an *ignis fatuus* of the mind,
Which leaves the light of nature, sense, behind. —[186]: A Satire Against Mankind, 1.11

Suggested by David Makinson

Huddled in dirt the reasoning engine lies,
Who was so proud, so witty and so wise. —[186]: A Satire Against Mankind, 1.25

Suggested by David Makinson

Ludwig Wittgenstein

⊢ 1889—1951 *Austrian philosopher*

Logic takes care of itself; all we have to do is to look and see how it does it. —[187]: §5:473

The logic of the world is prior to all truth and falsehood.

Logic must look after itself ... In a certain sense, we cannot make mistakes in logic. —[187]: §5.473.

Logic is not a body of doctrine, but a mirror-image of the world. Logic is transcendental. —[187]: 6.13

Logic deals with every possibility and all possibilities are its facts. —[187]: §2.0121

Suggested by Ilpo Halonen

W. Hugh Woodin

⊢ *American mathematician*

The current situation is the following:

We can build models of set theory with significant control over what is true in the model.

During the 35 years since Cohen's work a great number of set theoretical propositions have been shown to be independent. Further problems in other areas of mathematics have also been shown to be independent.

This, as of yet, cannot be accomplished for models of number theory. The intuition of a true model of number theory remains unchallenged. —[189]

24 X

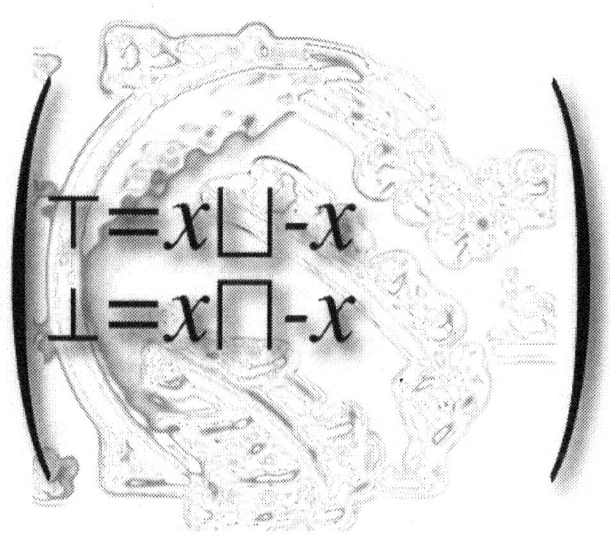

Malcolm X

⊢ 1925—1965 *American civil-rights leader*

I'm sorry to say that the subject I most disliked was mathematics. I have thought about it. I think the reason was that mathematics leaves no room for argument. If you made a mistake, that was all there was to it. —[190]

Xenophanes

⊢ ca 570—ca 480 BC *Greek philosopher*

The gods did not reveal from the beginning
All things to us; but in the course of time
Through seeking, men found that which is better.
But as for certain truth, no man has known it,
Nor will he know it; neither of the gods,
Nor yet of all the things of which I speak.
And even if by chance he were to utter
The final truth, he would himself not know it;
For all is but a woven web of guesses. —[191]

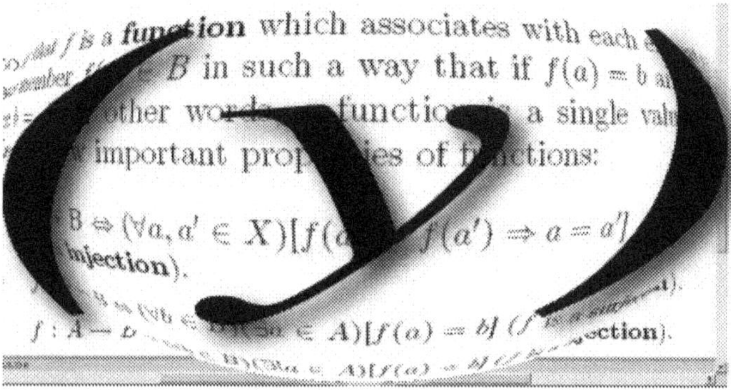

William Butler Yeats

⊢ 1865—1939 *Irish poet and dramatist*

People who lean on logic and philosophy and rational exposition end by starving the best part of the mind. —[193]

Though logic-choppers rule the town,
And every man and maid and boy
Has marked a distant object down,
An aimless joy is a pure joy ...
—[192]: Tom O'Roughley

Yes, Prime Minister

⊢ *English TV program*

He's suffering from Politicians' Logic. Something must be done, this is something, therefore we must do it.

Emile Zola

⊢ 1840—1902 *French novelist*

If you shut up truth and bury it under the ground, it will but grow, and gather to itself such explosive power that the day it bursts through it will blow up everything in its way.

Bibliography

[1] Addison, J. (2004). *Works of Joseph Addison.* West Midlands Creative Literature Collection.
http://www3.shropshire-cc.gov.uk/wmclc.htm

[2] Anderson, A.R. and Belnap, N.D. (1975). *Entailment,* vol. 1. Princeton: Princeton University Press.

[3] Anderson, M. (2002). *My Lord, What a Morning: An Autobiography.* University of Illinois Press, reprint edition.

[4] de Andreade, O. (1928). *Manifesto Antropofágico,* Revista de Antropofagia, n.1, ano 1, maio 1928. Translated as *Anthropophagite Manifesto.*
http://www.agencetopo.qc.ca/carnages/manifeste.html.

[5] U.S. womens magazine contributor. Weekly Visitor or Ladies Miscellany, p. 12 (1805).

[6] St. Thomas Aquinas (1998). *Selected Philosophical Writings: Posterior Analytica.* Oxford University Press.

[7] Aragon, L. (1991). *Treatise on Style/Traite Du Style.* University of Nebraska Press.

[8] Aristotle (2004). 'Aristotle's Principle of Non-Contradiction' in *Metaphysics,* Book IV, Part 3 & 4. Translation by W.D. Ross. A Philosophy of Reason.
http://www.apor.info/aristotle/pnc.htm

[9] Aristotle (2004). *Poetics*
http://classics.mit.edu/Aristotle/poetics.html

[10] Quoted in E.G.R. Taylor (1964), *Mathematical Practitioners of Tudor and Stuart England.* Cambridge: Cambridge University Press.

[11] Asimov, I. (1996). *The Relativity of Wrong.* New York: Kensington Books.

[12] Atkinson, J.B. (1972). *This Bright Land: A Personal View.* Doubleday.

[13] Bacon, F. (2000). *The Two Books of Francis Bacon: Of the Proficience and The Advancement of Learning, divine and humane* (*Collected Works of Sir Francis Bacon*). Classic Books.

[14] Barrow, J.D. (1992). *Pi in the Sky.* Oxford: Clarendon Press.

[15] Barry, D. (1997). *Dave Barry's Greatest Hits.* Ballantine Books, reprint edition.

[16] Barwise, J. and Feferman, S. (1985). 'Introduction,' in *Model-Theoretic Logics: Background and Aims.* Springer-Verlag.

[17] Bashevis, I. (2004). *Singer Collected Stories: Gimpel the Fool to the Letter Writer.* Library of America.

[18] de Beauvoir, S. (1989). *Second Sex.* Vintage, reissue edition, 1989.

[19] Beecher, L. (2004). *Plea For The West: The Works Of Lyman Beecher.* Reprint Services.

[20] van Benthem, J. (2003). 'Fifty Years: Changes and Constants in Logic,' in *Trends in Logic: 50 Years of Studia Logica*, edited by V.F. Hendricks and J. Malinowski. Dordrecht / London / Boston, Kluwer Academic Publishers: 35–56.

[21] Berenson, B. (1892). *Notebook. The Letters of Bernard Berenson and Isabella Stewart Gardner, 1887-1924: With Correspondence by Mary Berenson.* Northeastern University Press, 1987.

[22] Bierce, A. (1998). *The Devil's Dictionary.* Oxford University Press, reprint edition.

[23] Bohr, N. (1982). *Niels Bohr Collected Works.* Edited by U. Hoyer. Elsevier Science LtD.

[24] Boltzmann, L. (1947). *Populaere Schriften: Essay 19, Ludwig Boltzmann, Theoretical Physics and Philosophical Problems.* B. McGuinness (ed.). Reidel, Dordrecht.

[25] de Bono, E. (1994). *De Bono's Thinking Course.* Facts on File, revised edition.

[26] *Times*, January 3, 1984.

[27] Bourdieu, P. (1990). *The Logic of Practice.* Cambridge: Polity Press.

[28] Brown, R.M. (1989). *Starting From Scratch.* Bantam, reissue edition.

[29] Brönte, C. (1846). *The Professor.* The Literature Network.
http://www.online-literature.com/brontec/the_professor/

[30] Bruyère, J.d.l. (1970). *Characters.* Penguin Books. Translated by Henri Van Laun. Originally published by New York: Scribner & Welford, 1885.

[31] Burke, E. (1795–7). *The Revolutionary War 2. Ireland.* Edited by R. B. McDowell. Oxford University Press.

[32] Bush, George W. Quoted by Allan A. Metcalf, *Presidential Voices.* Houghton Mifflin, 2004.

[33] Bush, V. (1945). 'As We May Think.' The Atlantic Monthly.
http://www.cindoc.csic.es/cybermetrics/pdf/23.pdf

[34] Butler, S. (2003). *The Notebooks of Samuel Butler.* IndyPublish.com.

[35] Butler, S. (2004). *Hudibras.* Free Books to Read, http://www.freebookstoread.com

[36] Cambell, J. (1997). *The Lives of the Chief Justices of England: From the Norman conquest till the death of Lord Mansfield.* Gaunt.

[37] Carlyle, T. (2000). *Sartor Resartus.* Oxford University Press, new edition.

[38] Carnap, R. (1937). 'Logic', in *Factors Determining Human Behavior.* Harvard University Press.

[39] Carnegie, D. (1990). *How to Win Friends and Influence People.* Pocket, reissue edition.

[40] Carroll, L. (1895). 'What the Tortoise Said to Achilles,' Mind **14**: 278–280.

[41] Carroll, L. (1988). *The Complete Works of Lewis Carroll.* Penguin Books.

[42] de Carvalho, C. (1956). 'A lua vem da Ásia'. Unknown binding.

[43] Chang, C.C. and Keisler, H.J. (1977). *Model Theory.* North-Holland Publishing Company, Amsterdam / Oxford / New York, 2nd edition.

[44] Chesterton, G.K. (1908). *Heretics.* Christian Classics, Ethereal Library.
http://www.ccel.org/c/chesterton/heretics/heretics.html

[45] Chesterton, G.K. (1908). *The Man who was Thursday.* Christian Classics, Ethereal Library.
http://www.ccel.org/c/chesterton/thursday/thursday.html

[46] Chesterton, G.K. (1908). *Orthodoxy.* Christian Classics, Ethereal Library.
http://www.ccel.org/c/chesterton/orthodoxy/orthodoxy.html

[47] Quoted in *The Renaissance: A Certain World: A Commonplace Book*, edited by W.H. Auden. Viking, 1970.

[48] Christie, A. (1942). *The Moving Finger.* Signet Book, reissue edition.

[49] Churchill, W. (1942). House of Commons, December 17, 1942.

[50] Quoted in: Irving Klotz, 'Bending Perception, a book review,' *Nature*, 1996, volume 379: 412 (1).

[51] Coffa, J.A. (1983). 'Semantic Tradition from Kant to Carnap to the Vienna Station.' Orginally published in Kant, 'Wiener Logik,' *Kants gesammelte Schriften*. De Gruyter & Reimer, Berlin 1910–1983, volume 24: 843.

[52] Colton, C.C. (1822). *Lacon: or, Many things in few words, addressed to those who think*. E. Bliss and E. White.

[53] Comte, A. (2002). *Système de politique positive*. English translation: *The System of Positive Polity*. Continuum Publishing Group.

[54] Cooley, M. (1999). *City Aphorisms*. New York.

[55] Dac, P. (1972). *Pensées*. Le Cherche Midi Éditeur, Paris, cited in Foreword of *Reasoning Under Incomplete Information in Artificial Intelligence: A Comparison of Formalisms Using a Single Example*, by Sombe, L. (1990). Wiley.

[56] Dehn, M.W. in *The Mathematical Intelligencer*. Springer-Verlag.

[57] Depeche Mode (1990). *Violator*. Mute Records.

[58] Dewey, J. (1964). *How We Think*. Dover Publications, reprint edition 1997.

[59] Dijkstra, E.W. (1979). 'My Hopes for Computing Science,' *Proceedings of the 4th International Conference on Software Engineering*, Sept. 17–19, 1979, Munich, Germany. IEEE Press.

[60] Dostoevsky, F. (1998). *The Idiot*. Oxford University Press.

[61] Doyle, A.C. (1982). *A Study in Scarlet* (Sherlock Holmes). Penguin Books, reissue edition.

[62] Doyle, A.C. (2000). *Scandal in Bohemia.* Penguin Longman Publishing.

[63] Doyle, A.C. (2002). *The Complete Sherlock Holmes.* Gramercy Books.

[64] Drange, T.M. (1998). *Nonbelief & Evil: Two Arguments for the Nonexistence of God.* Prometheus Books.

[65] Ebert, R. (1993). Review of 'Searching for Bobby Fischer.' August 11, 1993. Rogerebert.com http://rogerebert.suntimes.com/apps/pbcs.dll/article?AID=/19930811/REVIEWS/308110301/1023&template=printart

[66] Einstein, A. (1950). 'On Science and Religion,' in *Out of My Later Years.* New York: Philosophical Library.

[67] Einstein, A., in *Life Magazine* 01/09/1950.

[68] Emerson, R.W. (1847). *Essays, First Series.* Borgo Press, reprint edition 1992.

[69] Figes, E. (1989), interview in *Women Writers Talk*, edited by O. Kenyon. Carroll & Graf Publishers.

[70] Firkins, O.W. (1990). *Oscar Firkins: Memoirs and Letters*, edited by Ina Ten Eyck. Unknown binding.

[71] Flew, A. (2001). *Merely Mortal?: Can You Survive Your Own Death?* Promethean Books.

[72] Forster, E.M. (1927). *Aspects of the Novel.* Harvest Books, reissue edition 1956.

[73] van Fraassen, B. (1980). *The Scientific Image.* Cambridge University Press.

[74] Frege, G. (1902). 'Letter to Bertrand Russell,' in *From Frege to Gödel — A Sourcebook in Mathematical Logic*, edited by J. van Heijenoort. Harvard University Press, reprint edition 2002.

[75] Frege, G. (1953). *The Foundations of Arithmetic.* Translated by J.L. Austin. Oxford: Oxford University Press.

[76] Frege, G. (1918). 'The Thought: A Logical Inquiry', reprinted in *Basic Topics in the Philosophy of Language*, edited by R.M. Harnish. Prentice Hall / Harvester Wheatsheaf, 1994.

[77] Friedman, H. (2004). 'On Foundational Thinking 1,' on FOM — Foundations of Mathematics. http://www.cs.nyu.edu/pipermail/fom/2004-January/007857.html

[78] Gabbay, D.M. (1999), reproduced from interview in *Logic, Language and Reasoning: Essays in Honour of Dov Gabbay*, Ohlbach, Hans Jürgen; Reyle, U. (eds.). Trends in Logic, Volume 5. Kluwer Academic Publishers

[79] Geach, P. (1991). *Peter Geach: Philosophical Encounters.* Edited by H.A. Lewis. Kluwer Academic Publishers.

[80] Goethe, J.W.v. (1984). *Conversations with Eckermann (1823-1832).* North Point Press, reprint edition.

[81] Graves, R. (1972). *Difficult Questions, Easy Answers.* Doubleday.

[82] Grillparzer, F. (1986). *Werke in sechs Bänden.* Deutscher Klassiker Verlag.

[83] Hankinson, J. (1985). *Bluff your Way in Philosophy.* Ravette Books.

[84] Hare, R.M. (1963). *Freedom and Reason.* Oxford: Oxford University Press.

[85] Harman, G. (1972). 'Is modal logic logic?', *Philosophia* **2**: 75–84.

[86] Hazlitt, W. (1839). *Sketches and Essays. By William Hazlitt. Now first collected by his son (The Complete Works of William Hazlitt (21 Volumes)).* Classic Books

[87] Heavside, O. (1990), quoted in M. Kline, *Mathematical Thought from Ancient to Modern Times.* Oxford University Press.

[88] Herbert, F. (1984). *Dune.* ACE Charter; 25th Anniversary edition.

[89] Hegel, G.W.F. (1969). *Science of Logic.* Humanities Press.

[90] Jaakko Hintikka in personal communication. Boston University, April 2003.

[91] Hintikka, J. (2005). 'The Continuum Problem and the Structureof The Second Number Class', *draft.*

[92] Hitchcock, A. in a headline in *Helsingin Sanomat* (the leading newspaper in Finland) in the 1960's during his visit in Finland.

[93] Herzen, A. (1921). *My Past and Thoughts.* Translated by Constance Garnett (1924-1927).

[94] Hoffer, E. (1951). *The True Believer: Thoughts on the Nature of Mass Movements.* Perennial Classics; 1st Perennial classics edition 2002.

[95] Hogan, J.P. (2001). *Code of the Lifemaker.* Baen.

[96] Hodges, A. (1983). *Alan Turing the Enigma of Intelligence.* London: Unwin Hyman.

[97] Hodges, W. (1998). 'An Editor Recalls Some Hopeless Papers,' *The Bulletin on Symbolic Logic*, Vol. 4, No. 1, March 1998.

[98] Holmes, O.W. (2002). *The Autocrat of the Breakfast-Table.* Akadine Press.

[99] Holmes, O.W. (1984). 'The One-Hoss Shay,' reprinted in *101 Famous Poems*, Roy J. Cook. McGraw-Hill, 1st edition, 1984.

[100] Hubbard, E. (1927). *The Note Book.* Kessinger Publishing, reprint edition 1998.

[101] Hugo, V. (1830). *Hermani.* Fredonia Books 2001.

[102] Human League (1984). 'Love Action (I Believe in Love)', *Dare.* Caroline.

[103] Huxley, T. H. (1874). *Animal Automatism.* Unknown binding.

[104] Introduction, *Journal of Applied Non-Classical Logic* **1**(2), 1991.

[105] Jones, R.F. (2004). *The Non-Statistical Man,* in *The Non-Statistical Man & Other Science Fiction Classics.* Pageturner.

[106] Kant, I. (1997). *Prolegomena to Any Future Metaphysics.* Cambridge University Press, reprint edition.

[107] Kant, I. (1920). *Critique of Pure Reason.* Edited by T.M. Greene. New York: Scribner.

[108] Keats, J. (2001). *Complete Poems and Selected Letters of John Keats.* Modern Library.

[109] Khayyám, O. (1859). *The Rubáiyát of Omar Khayyám.* Translated by Edward FitzGerald. Unknown binding.

[110] Kleene, S.C. (1967). *Mathematical Logic.* Dover Publications, reprint edition 2002.

[111] Daniel Kolak in *Neuroethics.*

[112] In *Jahresberichte der Deutschen Mathematiker Vereinigung.*

[113] In H. Eves (1972), *Mathematical Circles Squared.* Boston: Prindle, Weber and Schmidt.

[114] Leibniz, G.W.F. (1989). *Philosophical Texts.* Oxford University Press.

[115] Lillo, D.d. (1982). *Ratner's Star.* New York: Vintage Books.

[116] Locke, J. (1994). *An Essay Concerning Human Understanding.* Prometheus Books, reprint edition.

[117] Marx, M. (2001). Relation algebra with binders, *Journal of Logic and Computation,* **11**: 691–700.

[118] McCarthy, J. (2004). 'Freeman Dyson on Inexhaustibility,' on FOM — Foundations of Mathematics
http://www.cs.nyu.edu/mailman/listinfo/fom

[119] Melville, H. (1849). *The Piazza Tales and Other Prose Pieces, 1839-1860: The Writings of Herman Melville.* Edited by eds. Harrison Hayford, Hershel Parker, and G. Thomas Tanselle. Northwestern University Press, 1970.

[120] Mencken, H.L. (1984) *The American Mercury.* Garber Communications Incorporated, reprint edition.

[121] Milton, J. (2004). *Paradise Lost.* Online Literature Library.

[122] Minto, W. (1899). *Logic: Inductive and Deductive.* Scribner.

[123] Mitchell, R. (2004). *The Leaning Tower of Babel.* Richard Mitchell's Publications Online
http://www.csse.monash.edu.au/~torsten/ug/

[124] Montaigne, M.d. *1575 ESSAYS.* Translated by Charles Cotton.
http://oregonstate.edu/instruct/phl302/texts/montaigne/m-essays_contents.html

[125] Morgan, A.d. (1894) in *Transactions of the Cambridge Philosophical Society*, vol. X, 1864.

[126] Cardinal Newman. *History of my Religious Opinions.* Unknown binding.

[127] Nicholas of Cusa. (1997). *De Docta Ignorantia (Learned Ignorance)*, in *Nicholas of Cusa: Selected Spiritual Writings*, edited by H. Lawrence Bond. Paulist Press.

[128] Nietzsche, F. (1996). *Human, All Too Human.* Translated by J. Hollingdale. Penguin USA, reprint edition 1996.

[129] Nye, A. (1990). *A Feminist Reading of the History of Logic.* New York and London: Routledge.

[130] C.O. Oakley in *The American Mathematical Monthly*, 56, 1949.

[131] Baroness Orczy (1982). *Leatherface: A Tale of Old Flanders.* Darby Books.

[132] O'Reilly, J. (1982). *The Girl I Left Behind.* Bantam Books.

[133] Pascal, B. (1995). *Pensees.* Penguin Books.

[134] Peirce, C.S. (1958). *Collected Papers of C.S. Peirce.* Ed. by C. Hartshorne, P. Weiss, & A. Burks, 8 vols., Cambridge: Harvard University Press, Cambridge, MA., 1931–1958.

[135] Peirce, C.S. (1992). *Reasoning and the Logic of Things.* Recently published by H.L. Leitner and H. Putnam, Harvard University Press, Cambridge, MA.

[136] Perlis, A.J. (1982). 'Epigrams in Programming,' *SIGPLAN Notices*, September 1982, Association for Computing Machinery, New York.

[137] Peter, L.J. (1993). *The Peter Principle.* Buccaneer Books Incorporated.

[138] Pike, K.L. (1962). *With Heart and Mind.* Eerdmans, Grand Rapids.

[139] According to John 18:38.

[140] Pirandello, L. (1995). *Six Characters in Search of an Author.* Penguin Books.

[141] Port Royal (1662). *L'Art de Penser.* Also in Antoine Arnauld and Pierre Nicole. *Logic or the Art of Thinking.* Cambridge University Press, 1996.

[142] Pread, W.M. (1909). *Poems.* Houghton Mifflin Company, reprint edition.

[143] Quine, W.V. (1986). *The Philosophy of Logic.* Harvard University Press, 2nd edition.

[144] Quine, W.V. (1976). *The Ways of Paradox and Other Essays.* Harvard University Press, revised and enlarged edition 1976.

[145] Rand, A. (1996). *Atlas Shrugged.* Signet Book, 35th Anniversary edition.

[146] Rand, A. (1997). *Faith and Force: Destroyers of the Modern World.* Plume Books, reprint edition.

[147] Rumsfeld, D. (2004). Donald Rumsfeld Quotes. About.com.
http://politicalhumor.about.com/cs/quotethis/a/rumsfeldquotes.htm

[148] Russell, B. (1950). *Unpopular Essays.* Routledge.

[149] Russell, B. (1993). *Our Knowledge of the External World: As a Field for Scientific Method in Philosophy.* Routledge.

[150] Russell, B. (2004). *Mysticism and Logic.* Dover Publications, reprint edition.

[151] Santayana, G. (1956). *Character and Opinion in the United States.* Doubleday Anchor.

[152] Schlegel, F. V. (1968). *Selected Ideas (1799-1800).* Translated by Ernst Behler and Roman Struc, *Dialogue on Poetry and Literary Aphorisms.* Pennsylvania University Press.

[153] Scott, D. (1970). 'Advice on Modal Logic', in *Philosophical Problems in Logic*, Lambert, K. (ed.). Dordrecht: D. Reidel Publishing Company: 143–173.

[154] Shakespeare, W. (2004). *The Complete Works of William Shakespeare.* Classic Literature Library.

[155] Shaw, G.B. (1908). *Preface to Getting Married.* A Penn State Electronic Classics Series Publication.
http://www.hn.psu.edu/faculty/jmanis/gbshaw/Getting-Married.pdf

[156] Shaw, G.B. (2001). *Man and Superman: A Comedy and a Philosophy.* Penguin USA, reprint edition.

[157] Smullyan, R.M. (1988). *Forever Undecided (A Puzzle Guide to Gödel).* New York: Oxford University Press.

[158] Smullyan, R.M. (2002). *Some Interesting Memories—A Paradoxical Life*. Thinkers' Press.

[159] Smullyan, R.M. (2004). Unpublished manuscript.

[160] Smullyan, R.M. (2004). Letter dated 10/30/04 to Vincent F. Hendricks.

[161] Sontag, S. (2002) in *Sociological Perspectives*, vol. 24: **1**.

[162] Elizabeth Cady Stanton in letter dated November 28, 1890 (1922), in *Elizabeth Cady Stanton: As Revealed in Her Letters, Diary and Reminiscences*, vol. 2, by Theodore Stanton, Harriot S. Blatch. Ayer Company Publishing, 1977.

[163] Steinbeck, J. (1996). *The Winter of Our Discontent*. Penguin, reprint edition.

[164] Supertramp (1979). *Breakfast in America*. A&M Records.

[165] Tagore, R. (2004). *Stray Birds*. Kessinger Publishing.

[166] Talking Heads (1984). *Stop Making Sense*. Warner Brothers.

[167] Tarski, A. (1944). 'The Semantic Conception of Truth,' *Philosophy and Phenomenological Research* **4** (1944).

[168] Tennyson, A.L (1917). *The Ancient Sage* in *The Oxford Book of English Mystical Verse*, Nicholson and Lee (eds.). Oxford: Oxford University Press.

[169] Time Magazine (1965).

[170] Thoureau, H.D. (1906). *The Writings of Henry David Thoreau*. Houghton Mifflin.

[171] Trench, R.C. (1858). *On the Study of Words*. Manybooks.net. http://manybooks.net/titles/trenchrietext048stwr10.html

[172] Twain, M. (1962). *Letters from the Earth*. Greenwich, Conn.: A Fawcett Crest Book, reissue edition.

[173] Unpublished, known from oral tradition in Poland.

[174] Vauvenargues, M.d. (1746). *Introduction à la connaissance de l'esprit humain.* University of Quebec, Canada. http://www.uqac.ca/zone30/Classiques_des_sciences_sociales/

[175] Veblen, T.B. (1989). *The Place of Science in Modern Civilization and Other Essays.* Transaction Publishers, reprint edition.

[176] In free speech case Winter vs. G.P. Putnams Sons, 1991.

[177] Weyl, H. (1940). 'The Mathematical Way of Thinking', an address given by Hermann Weyl at the Bicentennial Conference at the University of Pennsylvania in 1940. It was first published in *Science*, 1940, volume 92: 437–446, and later reproduced in James R. Newman's *The World of Mathematics* (volume 3). Dover Publications.

[178] Hermann Weyl quoted in *The American Mathematical Monthly*, November, 1992.

[179] Whitehead, A. N. (1898). *A Treatise on Universal Algebra with Applications.*

[180] Whitehead, A.N. (1933). *Adventures of Ideas.* New York: Macmillan.

[181] Whitehead, A.N. (1938). *Modes of Thought.* New York: Macmillan.

[182] Whitehead, A.N. (1968). *Essays in Science and Philosophy.* Greenwood Publishing Group.

[183] Whitehead, A.N. (1959). *Introduction to Mathematics.* Oxford University Press, revised edition.

[184] Whitman, W. (1855; 1881). *Leaves of Grass, Song of Myself.* The Walt Whitman Archive http://www.whitmanarchive.org/

[185] Will, G.F. (1993). *Restoration.* Free Press, reprint edition.

[186] Wilmot, J. (2002). *The Complete Poems.* Yale University Press

[187] Wittgenstein, L. (1922). *Tractatus Logico-Philosophicus.* Translated by D.F. Pears and B.F. McGuinness. Routledge and Kegan Paul, 1961.

[188] Wittgenstein, L. (1977). *Vermischte Bermerknungen.* Frankfurt am Main: Suhrkamp Verlag.

[189] Woodin, W.H. (2001). The Continuum Hypothesis (I), *Notices of the AMS*, June/July 2001. http://www.ams.org/notices/200106/fea-woodin.pdf

[190] Malcolm X. (1987). *Autobiography of Malcolm X.* Ballantine Books, reissue edition 1997.

[191] Xenophanes (2001). *Xenophanes of Colophon: Fragments and Commentary.* Edited and translated by Arthur Fairbanks. London: K. Paul, Trench, Trubner, 1898. Hannover Historical Texts Project. http://history.hanover.edu/texts/presoc/Xenophan.html

[192] Yeats, W.B. (1996). *The Collected Works of W.B. Yeats Volume I: The Poems.* Scribner, revised second edition.

[193] Yeats, W.B. (2004). *The Collected Works of W.B. Yeats Volume IX: Early Articles and Reviews: Uncollected Articles and Reviews Written Between 1886 and 1900.* Scribner.

Contributors

- **Johan van Benthem** (The Netherlands)
- **Patrick Blackburn** (France)
- **Brian F. Chellas** (Canada)
- **Paul Dekker** (The Netherlands)
- **George Englebretsen** (Canada)
- **Leo Esakia** (Ukraine)
- **Dov M. Gabbay** (United Kingdom)
- **Paolo Di Gusta** (Italy)
- **Ilpo Halonen** (Finland)
- **Aaron Hunter** (Canada)
- **Daniel Kolak** (USA)
- **Muhammad Legenhausen** (Iran)
- **David Makinson** (United Kingdom)
- **Joao Marcos** (Brazil)
- **Stig A. Rasmussen** (Denmark)
- **Raymond Smullyan** (USA)
- **John Sowa** (USA)
- **John Symons** (USA)
- **Achille Varzi** (USA)
- **Jørgen Villadsen** (Denmark)
- **Dag Westerstahl** (Sweden)
- **Jan Wolenski** (Poland)

Acknowledgements

- Prof. Johan van Benthem
- Prof. Dov M. Gabbay
- Prof. Jaakko Hintikka
- Prof. Daniel Kolak
- Prof. Maarten Marx
- Prof. Raymond M. Smullyan
- Dr. Douglas B. Quine / Literary Executor, W.V. Quine Estate http://www.wvquine.org
- The Society of Authors, on behalf of the Bernard Shaw Estate
- A P Watt Ltd on behalf of The Royal Literary Fund
- A P Watt LtD on behalf of The Trustees of the Robert Graves Copyright Trust
- Kensington Books
- Oxford University Press
- Reidel
- North Point Press
- Fredonia Boos
- Random House Inc.
- Mute Liberation Technologies

- The American Mathematical Monthly
- Philosophia
- Classic Books
- Dodd, Mead & Company
- Transaction Publishers
- Scribner
- McGraw-Hill
- A&M Records
- Humanities Press
- Mind
- Modern Library
- Prentice Hall / Harvester Wheatsheaf
- Reprint Services
- Clarendon Press
- Carroll & Graf Publishers
- Pennsylvania University Press
- Gaunt
- The Atlantic Monthly
- Rogerebert.com
- Elsevier Science LtD.
- A Philosophy of Reason
  http://www.apor.info/
- Eerdmans
- Borgo Press
- Yale University Press

- Le Cherche Midi Éditeur
- About.com
  http://www.about.com
- Anagrama
- IEEE
- Classic Literature Library
- Ravette Books
- De Gruyter & Reimer
- Princeton University Press
- Nature
- ZAADZ
  http://www.zaadz.com/
- Ayer Company Publishing
- Prometheus Books
- Oregon State University
- ThinkExist
  http://en.thinkexist.com/
- Vintage Books
- Deutscher Klassiker Verlag
- Helsingin Sanomat
- Continuum Publishing Group
- Harvard University Press
- Pocket
- Christian Classics / Ethereal Library
  http://www.ccel.org/
- Houghton Mifflin Company

- Bartleby.com
  http://www.bartleby.com
- Richard Mitchell's Publications Online
  http://www.csse.monash.edu.au/~torsten/ug/
- The Walt Whitman Archive
  http://www.whitmanarchive.org
- Suhrkamp Verlag
- Free Books to Read
  http://www.freebookstoread.com
- Penguin Books
- University of Quebec
  http://www.uqac.ca/zone30/
  Classiques_des_sciences_sociales/
- North-Holland Publishing Company
- Northwestern University Press
- IndyPublish.com
- The Mathematical Intelligencer
- ACM Publications
- Buccaneer Books Incorporated
- Warner Brothers
- Prindle, Weber and Schmidt
- EMI Music
- Kluwer Academic Publishers
- University of Nebraska Press
- Vintage
- Hannover Historical Texts Project
  http://history.hanover.edu/

- Wiley
- University of Toronto Press
- Ballantine Books
- Darby Books
- Library of America
- Penguin Longman Publishing
- Signet Book
- Facts on File
- Farrar & Straus
- University of Nebraska Press
- Philosophical Library
- Penguin Group (USA) Inc.
- Life Magazine
- Manybooks.net
  http://manybooks.net/
- ACE Charter
- Baen
- Routledge
- AMS – American Mathematical Society
- Notices of the AMS
- Thinkers' Press
- Online Literature Library
  http://www.literature.org
- Paulist Press
- The Bulletin for Symbolic Logic

- The Association for Symbolic Logic
- Dutton Books
- Science
- Springer-Verlag
- Springer Science and Business Media
- ΦLOG
  The Network for Philosophical Logic and Its Applications
  http://www.philog.ruc.dk
- ΦNEWS
  The Newsletter for Philosophical Logic and Its Applications
  http://www.phinews.ruc.dk
- Gramercy Books
- Women Writers Talk
- Greenwood Publishing Group
- FOM—Foundations of Mathematics
  http://www.cs.nyu.edu/mailman/listinfo/fom
- Unwin Hyman
- Cambridge University Press
- West Midlands Creative Literature Collection
  http://www3.shropshire-cc.gov.uk/wmclc.htm
- Polity Press
- Dover Publications
- MIT Press
- Les Editions de Minuit / Irene Lindon
- University of Illinois Press
- Editions Gallimard
- Harvest Books

- Journal of Logic and Computation
- Journal of Applied Non-Classical Logic
- Harvard University Press
- E. Bliss and E. White
- The Literature Network
  http://www.online-literature.com
- Dutton Books
- Caroline
- Bantam Books
- Sociological Perspectives
- Association for Computing Machinery
- Fawcett Crest
- Macmillan
- Pageturner
- Garber Communications Incorporated
- Association for Computing Machinery
- Plume Books
- Doubleday
- Philosophy and Phenomenological Research

VINCENT F. HENDRICKS

⊢ 1970—

Vincent F. Hendricks holds two doctoral degrees in philosophy (dr. phil and PhD) and is Professor of Epistemology, Logic and Methodology. His professional interests focus on the intersection between formal and mainstream philosophy—especially as it relates to epistemology, logic and philosophy of science.

Vincent F. Hendricks is the author and/or editor of numerous books and articles on epistemology, methodology and logic. Among his most recent books are *The Convergence of Scientific Knowledge—a View from the Limit* (Kluwer 2001), *Modern Elementary Logic* (Høst & Søn 2002) and *Forcing Epistemology* (Cambridge University Press 2005).

In 2002 Vincent F. Hendricks founded ΦLOG—The Network for Philosophical Logic and Its Applications, and started the associated ΦNEWS—The Newsletter for Philosophical Logic and its Applications published by Springer.

He is editor (with Prof. John Symons) of *Synthese Library*, the highly estimated book series in philosophy and one of the editors of the reknown journal *Synthese—An International Journal for Epistemology, Methodology and Philosophy of Science* both published by Springer.

In 2005 Vincent F. Hendricks founded

$$\frac{\text{VINCE}}{\text{INC}}\text{.com}$$

a platform for promoting philosophy to a layman audience. As parts of this endeavor are the collections of pertinent, critical and humorous citations and aphorisms about philosophy and its broader intellectual environment, in particular the trilogy

FEISTY FRAGMENTS: FOR PHILOSOPHY

LOGICAL LYRICS: FROM PHILOSOPHY TO POETICS

500CC: ComputerCitations

published by King's College Publications, London.

THE TRILOGY

FEISTY FRAGMENTS: FOR PHILOSOPHY

⊢ September 2004

Feisty Fragments: For Philosophy is a collection of more than 550 quotations from people from all walks of life expressing their rather critical and often quite humorous takes on both philosophy and philosophers—from Nietzsche to Einstein, from Catherine the Great to John F. Kennedy.

> Funny, provocative, informative: this is a book for all those readers who want to learn more about philosophy, and for those philosophers who want to learn more about the world. —Achille Varzi

LOGICAL LYRICS: FROM PHILOSOPHY TO POETICS

⊢ March 2005

Logical Lyrics: From Philosophy to Poetics is a collection of citations and aphorisms from all sorts of people – from Napoleon Bonaparte to Human League – expressing their embracing, critical and humorous views on logic and logical matters.

> I found this collection utterly absorbing from beginning to end. It combines some very sagacious ideas with some choice bits that are delightfully funny. —Raymond M. Smullyan

500CC: ComputerCitations

⊢ September 2005

'hAS aNYONE sEEN MY cAPSLOCK kEY?' *500CC* records the experiences we have as computer users, abusers and Internet-cruisers—from rage and anger via joy, laughter and appreciation to despair and frustration.

> 500CC contains an amazing assortment of computer related quotes. It's the sort of book you put down and then simply must pick up again 5 minutes later. If you only ever buy two books about Computing, then buy this one twice and give one copy to a friend. —Kevin Warwick

Index

www.ingramcontent.com/pod-product-compliance
Lightning Source LLC
LaVergne TN
LVHW090943080826
845145LV00003B/863